The INTIMACY STRUGGLE

REVISED AND EXPANDED FOR ALL ADULTS

JANET G. WOITITZ

Health Communications, Inc.
Deerfield Beach, Florida

www.hcibooks.com

**Library of Congress Cataloging-in-Publication Data
is available through the Library of Congress**

The Intimacy Struggle © 1993 Janet Geringer Woititz
A revised and expanded version of *The Struggle for Intimacy*
© 1985 Janet Geringer Woititz

ISBN 13: 978-1-55874-277-2
ISBN 10: 1-55874-277-8

HCI, its logos, and marks are trademarks of Health Communications, Inc.

Publisher: Health Communications, Inc.
          3201 S.W. 15th Street
          Deerfield Beach, FL 33442–8190

Cover design by Larissa Hise Henoch
Interior formatting by Lawna Patterson Oldfield

Contents

Introduction

Everyone struggles with intimacy. Divorce statistics and the number of unhappy people we all know confirm that struggling with relationships is part of the human condition. If your family was dysfunctional in any way, you may have some very special problems and very special needs.

When I first wrote this book, I was addressing the needs of Adult Children of Alcoholics. As time went by, it became clear that the information was helpful and relevant for a much broader range of people looking for ways to make their relationships work and discovering that they had few skills. It was not easy.

Although the struggle for intimacy is not yours alone, for you the ways needed to fix the problems may be unique.

First, you were set up for the situation in which you now find yourself. You never had a chance to "do it right" because you've never experienced what "doing it right" looked like or felt like. It wasn't your fault if you always felt that other people knew some secret about successful relationships that you didn't know.

You may feel overwhelmingly guilty because you have been so ineffectual in your intimate relationships. Even if you learn nothing else from reading this book, please accept, right now, that you are not to blame for the pain you have suffered—and inflicted—to this point.

You didn't have an effective role model for loving relationships. You have had to make it all up. What you did know is that you didn't want to be like your parents, but you didn't know how to filter the destructive actions from the good actions. So you created a fantasy about how ideal relationships work from a fanciful blend of what you imagined, saw at a distance or observed on TV.

All of us learn to relate to others by watching how our parents interacted with each other and with their children. Take a minute before you read further to create a visual picture for yourself of the interactions you observed between your parents. Think how you related to your mother, to your father. Do not judge. Just look objectively at your childhood experiences as you remember them. No matter how different your relationship behavior as an adult may look, it is, in large measure, a reaction to those experiences.

You will learn better ways to interact with others as you read this book. You will have new options and choices. And you will have a new responsibility to choose the better ways.

I want you to picture the model for your adult relationships which you learned while growing up in a family where the needs of the adults came before the needs of the children. The following pages will give you a broad overview. Think about your own childhood and your own family as you read them.

Chemical Dependency: One Example of the Insidious Deterioration of a Relationship

Where did it go wrong? What happened? Who is responsible? Where is the sense? What does it mean? Where will it all end? Circles and circles and circles and circles—all filled with confusion. Where did we go off the track? Is it possible to understand?

For each couple the beginning is different. Even so, the process that occurs in the chemically dependent marital relationship—and it is important to recognize that there are many other dysfunctional systems that have their own patterns of deterioration—is essentially the same. For the starting point let's take a look at the marriage vows. Most wedding services include the following statements—for better or worse—for richer or poorer—in sickness and in health—until death do us part. Maybe that's where the trouble began. Did you mean what you said when you said it? If you knew at that time that you were going to have not the better but the worse, not the health but the sickness, not the richer but the poorer and the potential suicide, would the love that you felt have made it worth it? You may say so, but I wonder. If you were more realistic than romantic, you may have interpreted the vows to mean through the bad as well as the good, assuming that the bad times would be transitory and the good ones permanent. This contract is one that is entered into in good faith, so there is no benefit of hindsight.

The idealizing that takes place when marriage is entered into is not realistic. Everyone idealizes the relationship at this time, not just those who will eventually live with chemical dependence or other dysfunction. Everyone does. The difference is that in the chemically dependent or dysfunctional relationship, reality continues to be distorted and, little by little, the couple loses touch with what a happy marital relationship is all about.

If the statistics are accurate, and they probably are understated, then a very large percentage of you grew up in chemically dependent or otherwise troubled households. This is an important fact to be aware of because it means you probably had no idea how to develop a healthy marital relationship to begin with. Your early attempts to "do it right" were built on models that you had never seen or experienced. Rather, they were built on models that you made up in your own head. Thus, the fancifulness of the marriage vows played right into the notion of "It will be different for us than it was in my family."

Although the marital pattern created by alcoholism is discussed in detail here and will be used as the reference point throughout this book, it is important to reiterate that there are many other dysfunctional systems that have their own, similar patterns of deterioration. Workaholism is an addictive process which tends to alienate families. Workaholism occurs when the enthusiasm to work hard in order to save and plan for the future, experienced in the beginning of a growing marriage, deteriorates to the point where one partner is spending so much of his time at work, bringing home so much work and is talking on the phone so much of the time he is home that the other person feels deserted.

The alienation process here is slow and the rationalizations very strong: "I'm doing this for us." "It's not fair to come down on me when I'm only trying to earn a living." "I'm tired at the end of the day, too tired to go out socially or to sit down and have a conversation and you need to be more understanding." The spouse will feel very guilty and the resentment will build gradually. There is no time for intimacy here, and no model for children of a healthy, intimate relationship.

Another situation which is potentially perilous is a situation where there are economic reversals. If a family is used to a certain standard of living and then the major job is lost and that standard abruptly changes, the stress of those changes can be played out within the family system. Although one would want to be supportive and although a couple would want to bolster each other up during these times, the pressure can overwhelm.

Here again, name-calling and blame-finding can emerge: "It wasn't my fault I got fired." "If you knew how to keep your mouth shut you wouldn't have lost your job." "My father said you were a loser when I married you." In these situations, people may have to move frequently in order to look for paying work that can support the family. This means developing new friendships for the children as well as for the couple. This connects to difficulty with intimacy later in life because there is an underlying sense of not wanting to get close to avoid dealing with the pain of saying good-bye.

Sometimes illness strikes and a family needs to be very attentive to one of its members. When this happens, particularly when the sick person is one of the parents, children watch as all the nurturing and the caring in the family goes in one direction and one direction only while the other parent is largely left out.

Although there is no blame to be found here, the situation often results in an intense anger at the sick person that cannot be expressed because of how guilty everyone feels because they know they shouldn't feel that way. This situation is one that creates distance and confusion: "Why does this have to happen to me?" "I wish someone would take care of me for a change." "It simply isn't fair."

Another example of dysfunctional family patterns in this regard would include cocaine abuse. With a substance like cocaine, the initial breaking down of the family system has more to do with the profound expense of the addiction than it does with the impact of the drug itself. Other addictions along this line would include gambling and spending.

Holocaust survivors will tend to not trust anyone outside of the immediate family system and they program their children to feel the same way, thus limiting their world: "How can you be sure he's your friend? I thought John Smith was my friend and he was the one who turned me in."

Children of divorce are disrupted as well. Too often they believe that it was their behavior that created the problem. Not true. With the exception of some recent studies, the prevailing feeling has been that children of divorce take about one year to adjust. This is also not true. Frequently these children are used as pawns to play out the unresolved anger of the parents and become very confused as to how adults relate to each other. This sets them up for difficulties in their own relationships.

Patterns of emotional, physical and sexual abuse may or may not be involved with alcoholism. More often than not they are. While alcohol is not essential to this violation of intimacy, the patterns here are similar in that children grow up in a situation where intimacy is not experienced as a loving, sharing, supportive process except when it serves the purpose of the abuser. Many other dysfunctional systems follow a similar pattern.

So often someone walks into my office and tells me he has "done it again"—once again has screwed up what was such a very good thing with another person. Hearing these words only makes one thing painfully clear: the person who said them has very little understanding of what a relationship is all about. If you are in a relationship, you cannot screw it up all by yourself. There is another person involved. You both had a part in creating the problems.

If your reaction to these words is, "But, but . . . if I hadn't said . . . if I hadn't done . . . then he or she wouldn't have," my answer to you is that this truly has nothing to do with anything. All couples in all relationships do things that turn each other off and get the other person angry. But if you know what a relationship is all about, you put energy into working out the problems together.

Whenever I hear, "Things would be fine if only he would . . ." and what follows is not something that impacts the lifestyle but something that is just annoying, such as, "If only he wouldn't crack his knuckles while he watches TV." I know that the annoying thing is not the real issue.

The other part of the revelation behind the statement, "You have screwed it all up and it's all your fault," relates to a sense of being totally out of control and needing to control. It is unrealistic to think that if things are a mess because of your behavior, then you can change your behavior and everything will then be okay. But if you put the responsibility squarely on your own shoulders, then you will have the sense that you are not powerless.

To go for a reality check I may ask, "Did he ever criticize you? Did she ever complain? Did he ever do to you what you are doing to him?"

The answers are invariably, "Yes, but I let it go," or, "Yes, but I forgave her."

That's what people do who care about each other. So these unforgivable behaviors that are all your fault and have destroyed the relationship are nothing but a smoke screen to hide the real difficulties.

Regardless of the particulars, by the time help is sought, the expectations so lovingly expressed by those fanciful marriage vows have changed a great deal. For the partner who is chemically free, the sense of self and any satisfaction of personal needs is gone, replaced by a single overwhelming question and desire: "How can I help him or her?"

The sense of what one can expect out of the relationship has shifted. The relationship is no longer Camelot. It is no longer even person-to-person. Indeed, the level of distortion that has occurred is bizarre: "I will stay . . . because he doesn't beat me." "Because she doesn't run around." They will still then say, "But I love him!"

When as a therapist I respond to this declaration by asking, "Tell me, what is so lovable about him or her?" invariably there is no response. This is because the power of being emotionally stuck is far greater than the power of reason. I know this, but I plant the seed anyway.

Somewhere between the vows of everlasting wonderfulness and the acceptance of life as a horror story lies the reality. Somewhere hidden in the muck is the truth. The relationship didn't get distorted overnight. It started out on one end of the pendulum and landed on the other. Somehow the process was so gradual that no one saw it happening, and the middle ground went unnoticed.

If I ask, "What *was* lovable about this person when you decided to marry?" the response comes quickly. It is not unusual to hear answers like, "There was a strong physical attraction, and we could talk about anything and everything. He was my lover and my best friend."

These sentiments are sincere and important. It is important to recognize that people who start out as friends and lovers have something special. It is important, therefore, to recognize that chemical dependency affects everything. It turns lovers and friends into adversaries. Friendship is based on a number of things. It is based on mutual trust and honesty. It is based on the ability to communicate openly. It is based on a sense of understanding and being understood. The chemical— whether literal or the legacy of one of the other dysfunctional patterns described above—eats away at this friendship slowly but surely.

The erosion probably begins in the denial phase. At this stage the drinking is causing problems, but no one wants to face up to it. So the lies begin. First the lies to the self, and then the lies to each other. The dependent person will lie mostly in terms of broken promises. The chemically free person will lie to cover up. The trust begins to break down. True feelings are held back until they become explosive. The honest communication begins to dissolve.

The physical relationship is a good indicator of what is happening in the total relationship. The attraction may well continue through the denial phase. It will continue to be a way of sharing, even as the words become more difficult. No one has yet to come up with a better way of making up after a drunken episode.

Gradually, the interest in physical intimacy will decline on the part of the chemically free partner. The need to be less vulnerable will start to take over. At this point the sexual experience may still be technically satisfying, but the emotion is held in check.

As in all other aspects, the deterioration continues, and what was a warm, loving experience now becomes a power play and a means of venting anger.

"Go to bed with your bottle—not me!" "I can't stand the smell!" "You have to make a choice!" "Who needs *you?* It won't be hard to find someone better than you!"

The gap continues to grow wider. No part of the relationship remains unaffected.

The climate becomes confused and the open communication that existed before gives way to suspicion and anger. The underlying concerns are not addressed and the couple, even though they still care about each other, lives a distorted lifestyle. Both partners are being directed by the chemical—one directly, the other indirectly. One is addicted to the chemical—the other is addicted to the chemically dependent partner.

The relationship breaks down even further; if the chemical dependency got no worse, the damage to the relationship would be reparable. At this point it is possible to argue it out and, at the very least, clear the air. Feelings can be expressed and the lines of communication can remain open, but this is not simple.

This insidious illness does not stop here. It separates the couple still further. The chemically dependent partner stops developing emotionally. The chemically dependent partner no longer wants to deal with or confront problems, and a large part of any marital relationship involves making decisions and resolving shared problems. Where will we go on our vacation? Johnny is failing algebra again. Can we redo the kitchen?

And so on with the stuff that life is made of. These issues are no longer shared. The chemically free partner takes over more and more responsibility. The resentment grows deeper. The gap becomes even greater.

A saving grace during difficult times is the support of caring family and friends. This is true here also, at least for a while. But if they have not experienced what you are experiencing, the support will only increase the pain. If only they could understand. So the isolation of the chemically dependent couple becomes greater. They become isolated from other people, and they grow further away from each other.

And the sickness continues. The feelings shared are similar. The pain and the desperation are felt by both, but they blame each other. The guilt is felt by both, but the responsibility is placed differently. Once close, they are now strangers most of the time.

Occasionally, you will find yourselves in the eye of the storm, and you will be so grateful. The idea is that now the drinking will stop and all will be as it was. It is a shared belief. It is a shared deception. The reality is that the disease will progress. It will get worse. And so will whatever is left of your relationship.

The communication deteriorates into forms of anger. The inner feelings evolve into worry, fear, despair. The feelings are shared, but in isolation. The chemically dependent partner numbs the feelings, and the non-abuser is doubled over in pain—relieved only by anger and occasional fantasies.

The fantasy is that the drinking will stop and everything will be as it was in the beginning. The miracle of abstinence is the shared fantasy. Alcohol will lose its hold, and you will live happily ever after.

Somehow that is the greatest lie of all, and yet one of the most universally believed. The drinking stops. What does that mean in terms of the relationship? It only means that the focus is lost. It only means that the chemical is no longer the focal point. A huge vacuum now exists. Nothing else happens automatically. The trust that was lost does not come back just because the abuse stops. Just as a history of unfulfilled promises damaged the trust, a new history has to come into play in order to rebuild it. The lies may stop, but sharing makes one too vulnerable to be open at this point. The anger does not automatically go away because the drinking stops. The feelings that were repressed by the chemical may want to come cascading out. How terribly insecure—how terribly frightening. How hard to share these feelings and expect to be understood. The lines of communication have been cut off. You are two blind people without a road map.

Abstinence is not enough. A whole new relationship has to be built. The new starting point has to be different from the original starting point. The starting point this time is best served in learning how to solve mutual problems. It is best served in developing guidelines of how to talk *to* and not *at* each other. How can each be heard and understood? If the relationship is going to be healthy, it is going to require a lot of hard work. Building a new foundation will require careful and long attention. The attraction that enhances the beginning of a relationship is no longer present. The basis of the relationship now has to be firmly grounded in reality. If both parties are committed to working on it, it can be more than it would have been had the chemical not entered into the picture. If both people are looking for the same things, there is a great opportunity for mutual, as well as individual, growth. If not, the fantasy is over. The relationship is done. Abstinence is not Nirvana.

Chemical dependency destroys slowly, but thoroughly. Chemical independence can lead the way to build a healthy marital relationship. It's the only winning game in town.

CHAPTER 1

Who Do You Pick
For Your Lover?

I know no one who, when asked the question, "Are you interested in having a healthy intimate relationship?" will not say "Yes."

Difficult questions like, "Do you know what it is or do you know how to select a partner who will enhance you?" are met with crossed eyes. Generally, the response goes along these lines: "I know I want it, I don't know how to do it, but I do want to do it right. So I panic, because I want to feel close to another human being."

When I then ask, "Why do you want to be close to another human being?" the response is threefold: "One, so that I won't be lonely. Two, so that I won't feel unlovable. And three, so that I won't feel afraid. In other words, I want to be close to another human being so that I will not feel what I felt as a child and carried with me into adulthood."

In effect, what is being said is, "I want an intimate relationship to fix my childhood."

This is not good, this won't work and this can't happen. As a result, people who are in relationships often come into my office expressing the following feelings: "Everything is going wrong with my relationship. I know that it's all my fault. I try everything I know to fix it, but it doesn't work. I'm not even sure if I love him/her. Maybe I don't know what love is. I'm so confused."

Sound familiar? It should. It is almost verbatim the story I hear when an Adult Child of an Alcoholic or the child of a dysfunctional family enters therapy because an intimate relationship is souring. And the story is the same whether the Adult Child is twenty years old and in a first serious relationship or forty years old and the veteran of one or more failed marriages.

"It just has to be my fault. Relationships always go this way. I thought it would be different this time, but it wasn't. Maybe I'm better off alone."

Have you felt that way? We all have—and we've all said similar self-deprecating things while in the midst of a troubled or troublesome relationship.

Is it a "normal" way to feel?

That depends upon whether you are feeling that way because of the current circumstances or whether these are deep-seated messages which have become a permanent part of your self-image because they were hammered at you time and time again while you were growing up. In both cases the feelings are equally painful, but in the latter case they are more difficult to erase.

Read those opening statements again: "Everything is going wrong with my relationship. I know that it's all my fault. I try to do everything that I know to fix it, but it doesn't work."

Today you are saying those phrases about your relationship. The context may be new for you, but the phrases and the feelings are not. Once again you are experiencing the helplessness of your childhood and reacting to an "old tape." Nonetheless, the feelings are real and oh, so powerful.

Other familiar feelings also well up, including confusion, the sense of being stuck, the sense of being unable to change your destiny.

This is all part of being in an intimate relationship. It will drag out all things, old and new, that you have experienced and felt before. You will play it all out again. With work the process and outcomes will be different, but the struggle cannot be avoided. Even those who have not been affected by living in an alcoholic family find one must work to have a good and healthy relationship. You have plenty of company in the struggle!

To probe a little deeper into the nature of the struggle you are facing, it is important that you recall some of the early inconsistent messages you were given by your parents. Like it or not, want to believe it or not, these messages are still influencing you on an unconscious level throughout all aspects of your life. *To change your life, you must change the message.*

Awareness is the first step toward changing the message. The knowledge of how your current patterns were formed will begin to release you from the self-critical indictment which is such a basic part of your nature. Let's take a look at these double-bind messages and how they affect you today.

Parental Message #1: "I love you. Go away."

Sometimes your alcoholic or dysfunctional parent was warm and loving, sometimes rejecting and hostile. Although your non-alcoholic or more functional parent told you that you were loved, he was often so absorbed with worry and so irritable that you rarely felt loved. There was no consistency.

This is love as you understood it as a child and as you are still experiencing it. Ever wonder why you are attracted to that person who is warm and loving one day and rejecting the next? Ever wonder why the person who says he or she will call and doesn't seems more desirable than the one who is consistent?

If, by chance, you do become involved with a lover who is consistent, you find that sort of person very unsettling because you have no frame of reference for this kind of behavior. I am talking about the type of individual with order in her life, the person who can predict with a reasonable amount of certainty what tomorrow will bring. This is also someone who will behave, feel and think tomorrow much as she behaved, felt and thought today. The challenge to win the love of the erratic and sometimes rejecting person repeats the challenge of your childhood. You are grateful when the inconsistent person throws you a crumb, but get bored quickly with the one who is available all the time.

You are playing out your childhood all over again because the only consistency you knew was inconsistency. The only predictability you had was the lack of predictability. You lived your childhood on an emotional roller coaster. That is what you understand. Think a minute—how many times have you created a crisis in your relationship to get the energy flowing again and bring the relationship back to more familiar ground?

Even though this may be obvious to you on an intellectual level, bear in mind that it may take longer for you to truly feel this truth because you were conditioned at such an early age.

Parental Message #2:
"You can't do anything right I need you."

Here is another set of conflicting messages which you play over and over again. When you were a child, you could never meet your alcoholic or dysfunctional parent's perfectionistic standards, no matter how hard you tried. You were never good enough. And you truly believed that everything that went wrong was your fault. If you would have been good enough, things would have been better for your family.

Yet you knew you were needed, and that your parent couldn't get along without you. That was perfectly clear also. Since it was impossible for your parent to get along without you, even though you were so worthless, you would struggle until you could find a way to "fix" things.

As an adult, do you find yourself drawn to partners who are both extremely dependent and highly critical? Are you drawn to those who repeatedly put you down, although you know they can't get along without you? Do you continue to strive for their approval because on a deep level you believe that there would not be so much trouble in the relationship if you were only good enough? And do you know you can't keep letting down someone who needs you so desperately? Sound familiar?

Another setup.

"Yes, it's true that your mother did and said those terrible things. But you must understand that she was drunk."

The implications of this double-bind message are especially destructive to you when you are in an intimate relationship. Your unconscious tells you that if you can find an explanation for inexcusable behavior, you must believe that the behavior is excusable.

In the family system affected by alcoholism, the alcoholic is rarely held accountable for his behavior. More likely the child hears from the other parent, "What did you expect from a drunk?" Or, in early family recovery, "You have to understand that your father has a disease." The child hears the message that the parent can do whatever he wishes by simply using the excuse of drunkenness or alcoholism. "Your daddy had a stressful day. If you were better behaved, he wouldn't have to yell at you."

Now that you are an adult, you have become the most understanding person in the world when it comes to your loving relationships, right? In almost every situation you will find a way to make everything okay—certainly if SOMEONE must be at fault, you will take that fault upon yourself. You have learned how to understand, and you have learned how to take full responsibility upon yourself.

Therefore, when you are treated in a lousy way, you analyze the situation and don't allow yourself to experience any angry feelings. Understanding a behavior does not make it automatically acceptable. But you learned to accept bad behavior when you were a child and denied yourself the pain for maltreatment because you believed, "Your father wouldn't have done that to you if he were sober."

This statement also contains elements of control and elements of guilt. Here is the kind of thought pattern that runs through the mind of the child in the alcoholic or dysfunctional family system: "If I feel guilty, then I am responsible. And if I am responsible, then I can do something to fix it, to change it, to make it different."

Giving up your guilt also means giving up your sense that you have control over the situation. And, of course, loss of control is a disaster. You have grown up to be the perfect doormat for an inconsiderate person. Often you end up in a perfect give-and-take relationship—you give, they take.

Parental Message #3:
"I'll be there for you—next time. I give you my word."

The underlying message here is—forget it! So you learn how not to want so that you don't get disappointed.

Sometimes you unwittingly become the doormat for a partner who truly doesn't want to treat you that way. Often you become tired and resentful. You complain about having to do everything in the relationship—yet it is almost impossible for you to ask for anything for yourself. You want your partner to be a mind reader.

Your fear of asking for something and then not getting it is as unsettling as your fear of asking for something AND getting it! The first outcome reinforces your belief that you are too unworthy to deserve what you want, and the second possibility is so unfamiliar that you actually don't know how to react. Even a simple compliment may cause you great discomfort.

You deal with the whole situation by abdicating responsibility for your happiness. You decide that your partner should know what you want and act on it without ever having been told. For example, "If I have to tell him I want to go to the theater for my birthday, it proves that he doesn't really want to please me." Your lover is now set up so that you can decide he doesn't love you if he doesn't pick up whatever vague hints you may have sent his way. You'll only be happy with a mind reader, a fantasy hero who will automatically know how to please you.

Parental Message #4: "Everything is fine so don't worry. But how in the world can I deal with all this?"

Both of these messages come through. "Don't concern yourself—everything is going to be okay." Yet the underlying sense you got from your parents is that everything is NOT okay. The result is that you develop into a super-person by the time you become an adult. You can (and will) take care of everything. You are in charge. Nobody else around you has to be concerned about anything. You can manage. How often do you say the following things? "Don't worry, we'll take my car. I've got enough money; I'll pick up the food. I'll make the arrangements. Don't worry. It's not a problem for me!"

CHAPTER 2

What Is A Healthy Relationship Anyway?

"What does a healthy relationship look like? What does it feel like? How do I get one? How will I know if I have one?"

These are very important and real questions that need to be addressed. Wanting to be involved in a healthy, intimate relationship is a universal condition. And defining just exactly what "healthy" is, is a universal question.

You know you are in a healthy, intimate relationship when you have created an environment where:

1. I can be me.
2. You can be you.
3. We can be us.
4. I can grow.
5. You can grow.
6. We can grow together.

Essentially that's what it's all about. It's paradoxical that a healthy relationship frees me to be myself—and yet I don't know who I am because acquiring self-knowledge is a lifelong process. Although you may not have a strong sense of who you are, you recognize clearly when you are NOT being allowed the freedom to be you. It is clear when you are feeling judged. It is clear when you feel that you are walking on eggs. It is clear when you worry about making a mistake. In effect, the freedom to be you means that your partner will neither interfere with nor judge your process of being and becoming.

You offer your partner the same freedom that you are asking for yourself. And you accept your partner as he is, and do not try to use the power of your love to turn him into a swan. You do not get caught up in your fantasy of who you want him to be, and then concentrate on making that happen. You focus on who that person really is.

"I accept you unconditionally, and you accept me unconditionally." That's the bottom line. It does not mean that changes in personality or actions are undesirable or impossible—it merely means that you begin by accepting your partner as he or she is.

"We are free to be us." Each couple defines their own relationship built on shared values and interests. First, they must decide what they each value as individuals and then they can build a oneness out of their separateness. Some of their differences are unimportant and can be either ignored or resolved. For example, issues such as, "You always leave the cap off the toothpaste," or, "I hate church socials," can be worked out easily.

Other differences are significant and need to be worked out if the relationship is to remain healthy and survive. Examples of more critical issues are, "I don't want any children," or, "I'll never have anything to do with your mother again."

Many experiences are enhanced because the two of you are a couple. Enjoying together the beauty of a sunset, a walk on the beach, a well-prepared meal, are examples of the "us" that make a partnership desirable. I am enhanced when I have me, you have you and we also have us.

A healthy relationship creates an environment where I can grow. In this climate of support, I also encourage you to do the same. Through the directions of our individual growth, we develop together as a couple.

A couple also grows together by developing mutual goals and working together on ways to achieve them. Interestingly, it is the journey toward the goals, and not necessarily the goals themselves, which help the relationship grow. Whether or not you attain a goal is part of the process toward the next shared experience.

Intimacy means that you have a love relationship with another person where you offer, and are offered, validation, understanding and a sense of being valued intellectually, emotionally and physically.

The more you are willing to share and be shared with, the greater the degree of intimacy.

A healthy relationship is not a power struggle. The two of you don't have to think the same way about things.

A healthy relationship is not symbiotic. You do not have to feel the same way about all things.

A healthy relationship is not confined to a sexual relationship which must end in orgasm, but one that celebrates sharing and exploring.

CHAPTER 3

Intimate Relationships: Truth Versus Myth

You have been living with many myths generated and perpetuated by your family system. Because of this you put such enormous pressure on yourself that you wonder whether having a healthy, intimate relationship is worth paying the price.

You are torn apart by push-pull issues which may be illusionary to others, but are very real, and sometimes paralyzing, to you.

"I want to become involved. I don't want to become involved."

"I want to meet someone. I don't want to meet someone."

"I want to get to know you better. Please, simply go away."

These issues interfere with your ability to get what you want out of relationships. If you want to change this, there is a process to follow.

Your first step is to take a good, hard look at these myths. Acknowledge them. Reject them. Then replace them with what exists in the real world. This is by no means a small task because you have been living with these myths for a long time. They will not vanish over-night. Simply becoming aware of them is the place to begin.

Relationship Myth Number 1:

"If I am involved with you, I will lose me."

Relationship Truth Number 1:

In the real world, healthy relationships enhance the self and do not absorb it.

Underlying Feeling: Fear of Loss of Self

This fear is present because you never clearly established your sense of self while you were growing into adulthood. The early messages that you received from your parents were very confusing. The lack of clear messages forced you to create many of your beliefs and values rather than learning them through examples.

Because your parents didn't care for you consistently in all the ways that a child needs care, you have had to do a lot of self-parenting. This has left you with an inconclusive sense of who you really are. Your self-hood is still in the state of evolving and is easily influenced. Ideally, by the time one reaches adulthood the inner messages are much stronger than the outside influences. In other words, your decision making evolves out of what your knowledge and instincts tell you rather than out of what you are reading or being told at the moment.

For children of troubled families, reaching this state of confidence in your ability to make decisions and act upon them is not accomplished so easily. Someone (anyone) else's opinion often influences yours. So, if you have been working on being your own person, and having con-fidence in your decision-making skills, you may feel threatened by the idea of involvement with another person whose opinions and ideas will be important to you—and may influence you in ways you don't want.

Susan had been wanting to take Italian lessons all her life. She finally signed up for class on Monday nights at the adult school. Then she met Joe. On their first date, Joe expressed the opinion that the only way to really learn a language is to live in the country. The next week Susan dropped out of her Italian class and began to spend Monday nights sitting by the phone waiting for Joe to call. Although she knew better, she rationalized that it was not the right time for her to take the class.

Feeling that sense of insecurity about your decisions does not mean automatically that you are experiencing "loss of self." What it does mean is that you will need to check out many of your perceptions, opinions and responses more carefully to see where they are coming from. Checking things out this way provides valuable information for you. Your next step is to not automatically dismiss your opinions in favor of new input. Instead, think it over. Give yourself a little time to assess and consider the situation.

Doing so gives you three choices in every situation: You may maintain your original position, change your position or adopt an entirely new position which incorporates both your thinking on the subject and that of others. This way you will feel much more confident about the decisions that you make, and less threatened by other people's opinions.

Relationship Myth Number 2:

"If you really knew me, you wouldn't care about me."

Relationship Truth Number 2:

You probably aren't as good an actor or actress as you think you are. Your beloved probably already really knows you. And cares about you anyway!

Underlying Feeling: Fear of Being Found Out

You may constantly worry that the person you love would want nothing more to do with you if he or she really knew you. Although it's a little vague just who is that real and horrendous person you may be, you still feel the anxiety very strongly.

Charles had been told his whole life what a poor excuse for a human being he was, He had a good job, dressed well and people seemed to find him interesting and attractive. However, he was certain that this was all a facade and that his father was right. As a result he kept everyone at arm's length.

You try to stave off being found out by acting out your fantasies of how a perfect person would act. You try to behave as though you have your entire life in order and are totally problem-free. After all, the simply human real you with human frailties will never be good enough for someone you love.

This belief is not something you made up. Since childhood you have been told overtly and covertly that you are the cause of family difficulties. Getting close to a loved one will expose your dark side and cause that person to negate the positive side of you that they have loved until now.

Changing this belief as an adult begins with hard, cold logic. Think about it. Were you really powerful enough as a child to cause your family problems? Truthfully, you will have to answer no.

Relationship Myth Number 3:

"If you find out that I am not perfect, you will abandon me."

Relationship Truth Number 3:

Nobody is perfect. And perfection does not exist.

Underlying Feeling: Fear of Abandonment

If you come from a dysfunctional background, fear of abandonment is very strong in you and differs from fear of rejection. Adult Children of Alcoholics and many children of troubled families seem to be able to handle rejection and adjust to it. Fear of abandonment, however, cuts a lot deeper because of childhood experiences. When someone rejects you it means that they turn their back on you. This is painful, but that person is not where you are rooted. The abandonment you feel relates more to the time when your parents were inattentive and you felt so isolated that you believed you would either no longer exist or would die.

The child who experiences living with alcoholism or dysfunction grows into an individual with a weak and very inconsistent sense of self, as we have already discussed. This fragile self is a critical self which has not had the nurture it needed. It is a hungry self and, in many ways, a very insecure self.

These characteristics are caused by the fact that you never knew when, or if, your parents would be emotionally available to you. You only knew unpredictability and inconsistency. Once the drinking or the trouble began, you simply did not exist. From experience you knew your needs would not be met until the drinking episode and any accompanying crises were over. And there was no way to predict when this would occur. What a terrible, terrible feeling. No matter what you did to try to prevent it, it would happen anyway.

Some children living in this situation continued trying to get their needs met and others gave up entirely. Those children who gave up entirely are not as anxious to enter into adult relationships as are those who still hold onto the fantasy that maybe, just maybe, this time things will be different.

The constant fear, however, is that the person you love will not be there for you tomorrow. In an attempt to guard against losing your beloved, you idealize the relationship and idealize your role in the relationship. Your safeguard against being abandoned is to try hard to be perfect and service all the other person's needs.

Whenever anything goes wrong (and in life, things go wrong), and when there is conflict (and in life, there is conflict), the fear of being abandoned takes precedence over dealing with the pertinent issue which needs to be resolved. This fear is so great that it is not unusual for you to lose sight of the actual problem completely.

A typical example of this is illustrated by the argument that Mary (one of six children whose father is still actively drinking) had with her boyfriend. It erupted because he was paying attention to other women and Mary got angry. The boyfriend responded defensively, told her that she was being paranoid and the argument continued.

When he left, Mary's anger soon turned into a sense of panic.

"Oh my God! I'm sure I was wrong. Maybe I was overreacting. Maybe he doesn't care about me anymore. Maybe he's going to leave me now. After all, if I weren't so insecure, his behavior wouldn't have bothered me."

It was a classic example of feeling abandoned.

Within three hours Mary drove to her boyfriend's home, gave him a red rose and apologized for HER behavior. He accepted her apology and they made love.

As she recounted the story to me later, I asked her, "How did you resolve the issue?"

She looked puzzled at first, then said, "Oh, that!"

Her terrible fear of abandonment had completely erased the original issue from her mind. The problem itself was lost when the panic set in. Reducing the pain of her fear of abandonment became her primary goal.

In cases like this, the problem doesn't go away just because it is being ignored. It will recur—maybe in the same form, and maybe in a different form—until it is dealt with or until it becomes a significant underlying issue with the couple. Repressing the problem does not cause it to be truly forgotten.

Mary's problem also illustrated the fears of "loss of self" and "being found out."

Mary started placing all her emphasis on his reaction to the experience. Then she began to wonder and worry about his reaction to other experiences. She thought about him constantly, particularly at times when he was not being attentive to her. She focused entirely on him, what he thought of her and how she could keep from losing him.

What about Mary's needs? What about the fact that she simply did not want to experience the way he was ignoring her to flirt with other women? She started judging herself harshly for reacting to his behavior. And the woman who felt that reaction began to disappear, something Mary recognizes and hates in herself.

The next time I saw Mary she commented, "I tend to lose myself in every relationship in which I am involved! Maybe I should end it now."

Mary does not believe she is worth very much and is fearful he will discover that. She believes she can fool him if she is on her best behavior. This creates heavy tension in the relationship, but she is afraid to be open and honest. Now she begins to wonder whether she reacted appropriately, and says, "This is really my fault. If I were more secure, I wouldn't have been so upset when he paid attention to other women. My insecurities are getting in the way.

"If he knows how insecure I really am, he may not bother with me anymore. Perhaps it is just as well that we ended the argument the way we did. I want him to see me as a 'together' woman, not as a scared little girl. He wouldn't have anything to do with that scared little girl."

How long can Mary pretend to be somebody else? The truth of the matter is that he probably already sees the "scared little girl" aspects of her personality and is attracted to the whole complex person that she is. She probably doesn't hide her fears as well as she thinks she does—or would like to.

It isn't important whether Mary reacted to her boyfriend's behavior because of her own insecurities or because he was being somewhat obnoxious. It probably is a combination of both. What is important is that the couple can discuss the issue.

If she is insecure, she won't become more secure by denying these feelings. She needs to acknowledge these feelings and then have the relationship develop to the point where she feels more secure. If he cares about her the way he says he does, he will attempt to accommodate her feelings. It is just as important for her to recognize if he is not interested in accommodating her feelings and prefers to play. Lack of accommodation on a relatively minor issue may signal lack of accommodation on more significant issues which will arise in the future. If this is the case, this relationship may not offer Mary what she is seeking.

Relationship Myth Number 4:

"We are as one."

Relationship Truth Number 4:

In the real world, you are you and I am me. And then there is us.

Underlying Issue: Bonding

Chances are that you did not experience the bonding in your early years that children in more typical homes did, especially if your mother was the dysfunctional parent. You could not depend on your parents taking care of your needs in a consistent way. You could not depend on being held and loved to solve your fears and calm your hurts. You could not trust that your mother would nurture you when you felt badly, whether you were right or wrong.

This affects the way you become involved in intimate relationships and the intensity of that involvement today.

Chris, whose mother is a manic-depressive, was taking a course in group dynamics at a local college. She reported that she didn't fit in with her classmates because they were concerned with their struggle to break the bonds with their parents, while her life-long struggle was in trying to DEVELOP bonds.

It is important to understand the difference and recognize the implications for the early stages of a relationship. Adults who had many of their needs satisfied at home (many to an unhealthy degree!) are able to let an involvement develop slowly. The investment can take place slowly, along with the growth of trust.

If adults who are products of homes where bonding never took place invest at all, they invest at once, heavily and on a deep emotional level. They seize the opportunity for bonding and are deeply involved before they know what is happening.

In the early stages of a relationship, there is great intensity of feelings. The body chemistry that attracts you to each other is activated and both parties are super-attentive and super-involved. You understand this degree of intensity because it feels to you like the energy you experience in a crisis.

This is a time when both parties greatly desire fusion. You are on each other's minds all the time—the phone calls are frequent—the desire to be together is great. Emotionally, it is a very powerful time.

These early stages are probably more an "involvement" than a relationship. It is the playing out of a fantasy. You cannot sustain this intensity which is so appealing. This is just a dynamite beginning, not what a healthy relationship is all about.

Initially this is flattering to the new partner and the closeness feels good. Often the partner gets pleasure out of feeling needed and in fulfilling the needs of the love object. But after a while this begins to feel suffocating and starts to become a drain. Your partner, if healthy, will stop wanting to be devoted completely and exclusively to the relationship. Life holds other priorities as well. As a result, the aura of the ideal love evaporates and things begin to be put into perspective.

When life begins to normalize, the intensity decreases and the telephone stops ringing all the time. You feel let down and rejected. You feel that your partner no longer cares because he no longer desires to spend every moment with you. From your point of view, this feels like abandonment. It's the drunk vs. sober parent scenario once again. You feel the gaping hole inside you even more deeply than before.

Clutching at your partner will force him into the "I love you, go away" stance, even though your beloved still cares. If you continue to play out your script, you will set yourself up for what you fear the most: rejection and abandonment. Then you will feel very confused because all you wanted was a loving relationship, and you will think once again you picked the wrong person. The truth may be that you were asking unrealistic things of your relationship. It is important that you be very clear about what you want your relationship to fulfill within you so that you avoid this situation.

On the other hand, you may react by deciding you no longer care and leave the budding relationship. If this is your choice, it may mean you are "hooked" on intensity and have fooled yourself into equating intensity with the relationship itself. Or it may mean that you are terrified about beginning the process of getting to know and being known by another person. It's probably a little of both.

Relationship Myth Number 5:

"Being vulnerable always has negative results."

Relationship Truth Number 5:

In the real world, being vulnerable sometimes has negative results and sometimes has positive results. But it is the only route to intimacy.

Underlying Feeling: Vulnerability

Early on you learned that you were the only one who could be responsible for your happiness, and that other people could make you angry only if you permitted it. You learned that you were in charge of your feelings. This was essential and critical to your being able to survive emotionally in an alcoholic or dysfunctional household. But now you need to open up your feelings to others if you want to participate in a healthy, intimate relationship.

It seems to me that the IDEA of being vulnerable is really more terrifying than actually BEING vulnerable. This was underlined for me by the discussions which took place one Monday night in one of our group meetings.

Jimmy opened it up by telling how intensely sharing his feelings in the previous group meeting had affected him all week.

"I left feeling so vulnerable," he said, "and the vulnerability lasted all week. I tried to be alone most of the time because I was afraid what would happen if I were with others while I felt so open to devastation."

The other group members understood what he was saying and agreed with him.

"Hey, wait a minute!" I said. "What does being vulnerable mean to you people? And what are you talking about when you say that you are afraid to be vulnerable?"

One by one, every person there defined "allowing themselves to be vulnerable" as being out of control of their lives. They felt that someone else would then take control of their lives and do them damage. To them, there seemed to be no other way. Vulnerability meant loss of self, devastation, being powerless to prevent these negative things from happening.

"When I was child," Malone shared, "I was afraid that I would be killed if I let my guard down for even one minute."

To her, allowing vulnerability meant potential death. Although to the others in the group vulnerability didn't have exactly that meaning, it did have another terrible meaning. It represented being left out, being hurt. In fact, just *talking* about feeling vulnerable created a very tense and somewhat depressing climate within the group.

"This is a very important thing for us to examine," I said. "If we are to develop healthy, intimate relationships, we must allow our partner access to our feelings. There is no other way to do it. If you are too terrified of being vulnerable and its consequences to take a risk, you are automatically saying that you are incapable or unwilling to have a healthy, intimate relationship.

"Have you ever considered the possibility that many of the feelings you are defending against are feelings which would actually enhance your life?" I continued. "Have you considered the fact that there are many aspects of love feelings that you haven't yet felt? That there are feelings of excitement about being in another's presence that you don't feel? That there are supportive feelings that you don't allow yourself to feel? Have you considered that there is a whole spectrum of feelings you have denied yourself because your terror about being vulnerable takes control of your life?"

Leslie shared that after three years she is able to be emotionally accessible to the man she loves. "I no longer have any secrets, emotional or otherwise," she said. "I tore down my walls little by little. Sometimes I've rebuilt a piece of them because I became afraid or because he didn't react the way I had hoped he would. But, slowly and gradually, I was able to let down the barriers as our relationship grew and our trust developed.

"I don't know many others that I would trust in this way," Leslie went on, "but I do know that it has not been harmful to me to be vulnerable in this relationship. It has, in effect, made me stronger. Once I really allowed him into my life, he could begin helping me feel things about myself which had been a struggle to feel before. And those new experiences help me feel more solid, more secure as a person.

"It hasn't been easy, but it has been worth the struggle!"

This reinforced for the group that the idea of being vulnerable may be more terrifying than the actual experience. In reality, you wouldn't even be reading this book if you were not interested in personal growth. Growth does not take place unless we allow access to new thoughts, feelings and ideas. And this access is gained only by being open to it, which means allowing ourselves to be vulnerable.

Relationship Myth Number 6:

"We will never argue or criticize each other."

Relationship Truth Number 6:

In the real world, couples argue from time to time, and are critical of each other's behavior.

Underlying Feeling: Anger

Children from troubled families believe that in an ideal relationship there will be no conflict and no anger. Although they recognize intellectually that this is impossible, emotionally this is what they want. Anger is very complicated and very much misunderstood by them. Historically, anger needed to be repressed. Children growing up in troubled environments live in a very angry climate where that feeling is never resolved. Expressing anger is never useful and only tends to make life worse. It never did anyone any good.

Therefore, you learn how not to be angry. Instead, you rationalize, explain things away and finally become depressed.

The words you use to describe your depression are words of anger. Since your anger was repressed, the only time it comes out is when it is no longer containable and has turned into rage. Rage is frightening to you because you don't know what you might do while you are feeling the emotion. This is because you have no experience in expressing the emotion.

Therefore it is not unusual for you to say, "I am terrified of allowing myself to be angry because if I lose control of my anger, I might kill." Many of you turn this anger inward, and since you would never harm others, you have suicidal thoughts. Chronic depression is also characteristic of children from dysfunctional backgrounds for a whole variety of reasons, some of them even biochemical.

You also fear another person's anger being expressed toward you: anger may cause physical violence, which must be avoided at all costs. This is another submerged issue which comes into play in a relationship. Yet there is no way to have a good relationship without resolving conflict. If two people are healthy and alive, and have thoughts and ideas, there will be times when they disagree. There will also be times when one person does something that irritates the other and makes him angry. It is impossible to know in a developing relationship where all the sensitive spots are. The ideal is to talk it over when anger surfaces, learn where it comes from and learn how not to repeat it.

Children from troubled families often translate anger into something that it is not. It goes something like this: "If I am angry with you, I don't love you. If you are angry with me, you don't love me. Since I do love you, then I can't allow myself to be angry at you. If you really love me, you will not be angry at me either." On an emotional level, this is the message you give yourself. Though not a valid message, it plays out just the same: "If I cannot contain my anger at you, I must reject you. If you do not contain your anger at me, then you must reject me." Once again the issue that made the couple angry has been forgotten. Why even bother to deal with it if the outcome will be rejection?

In addition, Adult Children have no experience in problem-solving with another person. You don't know how to resolve the angry feelings.

You don't know how to work with their anger in order to dissipate it. Anger needs to be expressed in one way or another. It needs to be recognized, acknowledged, talked over, understood and dissipated. It is important to realize that anger is an ever-present, hidden issue in your relationships.

Part of what made Mary, the woman whose story was told earlier in the chapter, believe her boyfriend was going to abandon her, or that she had to reject him, was her anger. Since she did not understand how to resolve anger, these were the only alternatives she saw.

In addition to being terrified at the depth of their anger, Adult Children are also uncertain about its appropriateness. "Would that make a normal person angry?" is the question I often hear. It is asked in reference to both the questioner's own anger and that of the people with whom he is involved.

"Just what is okay to be angry about?" the Adult Child wants to know.

Recently, I gave a lecture on Adult Children and a client and her boyfriend attended. He said, "I came because I want to know as much as I can about the things that have affected Carol because I love her." I was most impressed.

They sat on the right side of the room and most of the rest of the students sat on the left. About one-half hour into the lecture, a security guard walked into the room, looked at everyone sitting there and turned out the light. I made a comment to the guard and he turned it back on and left the room. I made light of my annoyance and went on with the lecture. The next time I saw Carol, she told me how furious Bill had become over this minor and transitory incident. "How could anyone walk into a room, look directly at us and turn out the light? The discourtesy was outrageous!" Bill had fumed.

Meanwhile Carol replied, "You know, it didn't bother me at all. I guess I'm used to being treated as if I don't exist."

For, this couple, Bill's anger was an important learning experience. It was clear to her that she needed to work on her own feelings of self-worth. Meanwhile, he learned how deep the lack of validation is for people with backgrounds like Carol's. Asking the question about whether the reaction was "normal" was what prompted the insight.

Who is to say what is normal? You react according to your history, and when your reactions are put into perspective, you decide what is normal.

Conflict does not mean if I win you lose or if you win I lose. We can respect each other and still not always perceive the world in the same way. We can be angry with each other and still love each other.

Relationship Myth Number 7:

"Anything that goes wrong is my fault. I am a terrible person."

Relationship Truth Number 7:

In the real world, some things that go wrong are your fault. Some things are not. Terrible things happen, but you are not terrible.

Underlying Feelings: Guilt and Shame

Guilt and shame emerge in any relationship with someone who has grown up with alcoholism or dysfunction. They are issues which need to be worked on. Ernie Kurtz, in his booklet, *Shame and Guilt: Characteristics of the Dependency Cycle*, describes guilt as "a feeling of wrong-doing, sense of wickedness, 'not good.'" The child is taught that what goes wrong is his fault. Even if it wasn't his fault he hears, "If you were not such a rotten kid, I would not have to drink." The guilt that many of you have is on a level so deep that you believe that your very existence caused the problem.

Shame, although somewhat different, is very closely linked to guilt, and one tends to feed off the other. Dr. Kurtz describes shame as "a feeling of inadequacy, sense of worthlessness, 'no-good.'" Guilt is associated with behavior, while shame relates to the essence of the person, the self, which is even more basic to the person. It is very hard to overcome these feelings. It is a life-long struggle to feel that your behavior is not "no-good"; it is also a lifelong struggle to believe that you are not "no-good."

In a relationship, anything that goes wrong becomes, to some degree, your fault. You feel it is your fault because the things you do are no-good and because you are no-good. It is your fault because in growing up it was the only means of control you had. If you were responsible for what happened, then you believe you could do something to change it. It was, of course, futile because you were not responsible; but the struggle to try made you feel that you were not completely out of control. In a relationship, if something occurs about which you feel responsible, you think you can do something to change it. You can apologize, or you can do something different. If you are guilty, then you can do something. If you are not guilty, then you are, because of your mind-set, in a very real sense, stuck.

Gloria was in a relationship with Eduardo. Eduardo took no responsibility for anything in the relationship that went wrong. When he ran out of gas on the way to her house, he told her that if she wasn't so insistent that he be there on time, he would have noticed that he was low on gas and wouldn't have had the problem in the first place. Since Gloria was so used to being at fault, she immediately apologized for having caused Eduardo this inconvenience. He forgave her as long as she didn't do it again. Since things were now peaceful, she did not have to look at the fact that his position was at the very least absurd, and at the very most abusive.

The idea of saying to your partner, "Why don't we take a look at this, regardless of whether I'm at fault or you're at fault. I'm okay and you're okay, and you and I need to find out what's going wrong," does not enter your mind. Because, essentially, you do not believe that you are okay. Even if what you did was okay, you don't realize it. Therefore, every interaction gets extremely complicated. Also, you do not want the person with whom you are involved to find out how inadequate or worthless you are. This, in turn, creates a climate in which you are less than totally honest. It goes back to the fear of being found out.

Relationship Myth Number 8:

"In order to be lovable, I must be happy all the time."

Relationship Truth Number 8:

In the real world, sometimes people are happy, and sometimes they are not.

Underlying Feeling: Depression

Many Adult Children of all types are what we call "chronically depressed." This means that there is an edge of sadness about them all the time. As I discussed earlier, it results, in part, from the anger they have turned inward upon themselves. It also has to do with the experience of loss. Chronic depression is also characteristic of kids from other dysfunctional backgrounds for a whole variety of reasons, some of them biochemical.

The Adult Child never got to be a child. He did not have the experience of being spontaneous, foolish, child-like—he did not have the experience of doing the things that children normally do. He did not have an opportunity to experience fun, or even to know what fun is. Although he knows what it is to be worthless or impulsive, the experience of having fun is something that, if experienced at all, is negligible. This causes a degree of sadness, which makes it harder to feel free and spontaneous in any relationship. This causes depression. The Adult Child will fight against depression because he tries to be pleasant in an attempt to be "the perfect partner"; but, for many, the feeling of depression is always present beneath the surface.

Loss is also a major issue with many of you. You have, in effect, lost your childhood and, therefore, many of the experiences other children have along with it. So for you, any change involves a loss of what you had before. Change is difficult because, psychologically, change means anarchy. With the fear of abandonment comes the fear of loss, accompanied by the ever-present fear that the relationship will not last. And if it does not last, once again loss will have to be experienced. This fear causes a tremendous conflict: "I know it won't last, so I wait for the bomb to drop, and I panic at having to experience the loss, so I hold on tight." This kind of behavior tends to drive the other person away, which sets the dreaded fears in motion. Unfortunately the feelings are not discussed, so there is little opportunity to begin to solve them.

The typical attitude is: "So that you do not see the level of my pain and how close it is to the surface, I will put on a 'happy face.' The song from *The King and I* about whistling a happy tune is my way of life." Elena had been unhappy and withdrawn for several weeks and refused to talk about it. Phil was certain that it had to do with him and became more and more anxious. He insisted that they both come in and talk to me. When they did, Elena broke down and cried.

"I found a lump on my breast," she sobbed. "And I'm terrified that if there is something seriously wrong with me, Phil will leave me."

It turned out that Elena was afraid that all she had to offer Phil was her physical attractiveness, and that if she should be scarred in any way that he would be repulsed by her. This is because when Elena was growing up, her parents told her, "You're lucky you're good-looking because you don't have any brains or personality."

When this finally came out into the open, Phil's first response was one of huge relief that he had not caused her pain and unhappiness.

Next he felt angry that she didn't trust him. And lastly, he was able to support, comfort and be there for Elena regardless of the outcome.

Meanwhile, Elena was able to learn that reaching out did not cause Phil to leave her. Instead, it gave her a new opportunity to share in their relationship on a deeper level. The two of them agreed that there was nothing so terrible that they could not tell each other about it. And when he asked her, "Wouldn't you want to know if I was concerned about my health? Wouldn't you consider it almost your right to have that information?" She said, "Yes, absolutely."

Since just wanting to be different doesn't make you different, Phil and Elena then talked about how to keep this pattern from occurring again in the future. One of the things they decided was that in their relationship, "I don't want to talk about it" is not an acceptable answer. They decided that "I don't want to talk about it now" can be acceptable if the question "If not now, when?" is answered.

Relationship Myth Number 9:

"We will trust each other totally, automatically and all at once."

Relationship Truth Number 9:

In the real world, trust builds slowly.

Underlying Issue: Trust

It is natural for children to trust others. From infancy, they trust that their needs will be met. If this early trust is denied, they die, as they are completely helpless and depend on others for nurture and care. Trust is so natural to children that even in a typical family they must be taught when not to be trusting. Children must be taught not to go with strangers, that it is not safe to run into the street, or to touch the stove. Children, in their naïveté, want to love and trust all people and all things.

In a troubled home, the child's needs are not necessarily totally unmet, but they are inconsistently met. This means that trusting people will mean being hurt, and therefore that trust is inappropriate. It means that the child must learn how to take care of himself. In order to survive, the child learns how not to trust, that he can depend only on himself. If someone is trustworthy, it is the exception rather than the rule. When there is an expectation, it is most often met by frustration and disappointment. "Don't trust" is something that the child learns very early and very well. However, it is contrary to the child's nature. It is an adaptive response to a maladaptive situation.

The discussion here is about how to build a healthy relationship. A major element—a necessary prerequisite for a healthy relationship—is trust. Without it, the relationship cannot prosper; it simply will not develop and grow. Trust is not easy to accomplish because you have to unlearn many negative responses and feelings to do it. You have to go all the way back to your early childhood and once again begin to trust.

In a group of Adult Children, a young man named Lawrence said, "I have just started a new job. I like everyone I have met so far, but I am not going to trust anybody just yet. They are going to have to earn my trust."

The group agreed with him.

I said, "Why not trust everyone and then discount those who violate your trust? It will take much less energy. It doesn't mean you have to act in any particular way. If you decide to trust, you don't have to behave any differently than if you decided not to trust. It would just make it easier for you."

The group was fascinated and wanted to learn more about this approach which was a new one for them. "It costs you nothing to trust automatically," I said. "You end up at the very same place. If you don't trust and someone behaves in a manner that is untrustworthy, then you have affirmed and reinforced the fact that you can't trust anybody. If you do trust someone and he turns out not to be worthy of it, yes, you will be disappointed, but you will not be devastated. Disappointment is something that you have learned to handle very well. Affirming the fact that it was a good idea not to trust in the first place does not mean you will not be disappointed. That is the reality of it."

This was a very curious idea to them—something, given their backgrounds, they could not have thought of on their own.

What does trust mean in a relationship? There are several components. First, trust means that your partner will not abuse your feelings, and that you will show your feelings. Right there you are stymied as you are already entering into an arena outside your range of experience. Trusting others is one of the primary things you have guarded against since childhood, and now I am telling you that it's not going to work anymore.

One of the things that makes a good, healthy relationship so scary is that trusting is the opposite of what you have learned to do. You must trust that the person you care about will not want to hurt you, and you must show some of yourself. This is the beginning of getting to know someone in a very real way. Trust also means that you will not abuse your partner's feelings and that he will be able to show them to you. It goes both ways.

Secondly, trust means honesty: the other person will say what he means and mean what he says, and you will do likewise. Honesty allows you to trust the other person not to lie to you deliberately. When you reciprocate, this helps give substance to your relationship. You will know when you reach out that your hand will touch a solid arm belonging to someone you can depend on. Your relationship won't be "fly-by-night," and you won't be confused.

Third, trust means that your partner will not willfully hurt you, and that you will not willfully hurt him. If it does happen, you will want to discuss ways to make sure it doesn't happen again. We cannot always know, when getting to know another person, what will be hurtful. It is extremely important to be able to say, "It hurt me when you said that," and for the other person to say, "It's important for me to know that; I don't want to hurt you. I will try hard not to let it happen again."

For many, trust means the promise of no physical abuse. I get angry every time I hear that an adult had such terrible childhood experiences that when we talk about trust it automatically means they want to be rid of the fear of physical violence. Physical abuse is inexcusable in any relationship, Therefore, it is non-negotiable.

Fourth, trust means the freedom to be yourself without being judged. It means that you do not have to walk on eggs, that you can be who you are, and that the other person can be who he is. You are both okay. Not judging yourself, and not being judged, is a whole new experience, glorious and exhilarating. It is also scary as hell.

Fifth, trust means stability. There is a certainty about the other person and about the relationship. It means that tomorrow's behavior will be similar to yesterday's, that you can count on things and that you can plan in advance. It means you know that if on Monday you make arrangements to go somewhere on Saturday, when Saturday comes you will be able to do it. Stability, being very inconsistent with your childhood experiences, may be difficult to learn and to accept in another person.

Sixth, trust means commitment to the relationship to the degree that the couple has agreed to be committed to the relationship. If your partner has said, "I will see only you; you are the only one with whom I am going to bed," you need to be able to believe it.

Likewise if you have offered the same thing, you need to behave accordingly. If you are to feel comfortable in a relationship, it is important to feel sure that agreements will be kept.

Lastly, trust means that confidences will be kept. You won't have to worry about anyone else knowing your secrets. Neither will you share the secrets of your partner. It is especially important, when you have an argument, to know that these confidences will not be used against you.

Because trust is different for different people, in addition to these seven points it can also mean whatever a couple decides it means to them, individually and together.

Marlene is an emergency room surgeon in an inner city hospital. Her job is challenging and tough even while it is rewarding, and once in a while she comes home feeling as if she's been sleep-deprived and punched repeatedly in the stomach. But she knows that when she's not feeling well, Hal's response will be, "What can I do for you?" It can be 2:00 PM or 4:00 AM when she wakes him out of dead sleep, but she knows that whenever she does, he will be a great source of comfort and security. One day when she got back from the hospital, she went up into the Jacuzzi he had made and he brought her up brunch and just sat by the tub. She can trust that he will be available to her, and because they've been together for so long, she also knows she can say to him, "I need to be in my own space," and he will honor that, too.

This wasn't always so automatic with Marlene and Hal, It is something that they have worked on and discussed over the years—how to be there for each other in ways that are non-intrusive but supportive. In Marlene's first marriage, her husband was never there for her, and if she was in need he'd be abusive. As a result, during the early years of their relationship, she would always arrange to have a backup, somebody else she could call upon so that when, inevitably, he let her down, she wouldn't fall flat on her face. Hal never let Marlene down, but it took her years to be able to trust that. It's something she had to work on consciously. She worked on it by being aware that she needed to work on it. And that works.

The facets of trust I have discussed here, although essential to a healthy relationship, are difficult to build. Trusting another person doesn't happen overnight, and you needn't criticize yourself because you find it difficult. Perhaps one of the easiest ways a couple can begin to trust each other is to discuss the difficulties they have with trust and acknowledge that it is something to aim for, You need to commit yourselves to working on trust on a step-by-step basis as the relationship develops. It is very important for you to recognize that trust is not something you can give automatically to another person in the depth that has been discussed here. It is important for you to know that developing trust is an essential part of the process of building a healthy relationship. At this stage, you may only hear the words and not have any idea of how to put them into practice. This is not unusual, but eventually you will learn to trust.

Relationship Myth Number 10:

"We will do everything together—we will be as one."

Relationship Truth Number 10:

In the real world, couples spend time together, alone and with friends.

Underlying Issue: Boundaries

Children of dysfunctional families have difficulty respecting the boundaries of others and recognizing what their own boundaries are. You grew up in an environment where boundaries were very confusing. It was difficult to identify the respective roles of mother and father. It was hard to know if you were a child or the mother or the father.

This confusion raises many questions. Whose pain did you feel? Was it yours? Was it your mother's? Was it your father's? Where did you end and somebody else begin?

What about privacy? What things belonged to you and could not be violated? Was your privacy invaded, even in the bathroom?

What are the limitations of good taste? What is appropriate behavior? What is inappropriate behavior?

Now that you are an adult, how do you decide if you are doing something reasonable, or violating someone else's rights?

Perplexing statements and questions often come up in discussions with Adult Children.

"He hugged me. I felt violated. Am I wrong to feel that way?"

"I let myself in because her door was unlocked. Why did she get so bent out of shape?"

"I enjoyed the evening and invited him in for coffee. What right did he have to move in on me on the first date?"

"I worry that I will offend you. I always say the wrong thing."

"I get all bottled up when I'm asked something personal. Isn't that my business?"

There is much confusion about what is intimacy and what is an invasion of boundaries. A lot of checking out is in order before you act. For example, don't do me a favor by cleaning my room unless you know I would consider it a favor. Don't insist on paying the bill after I've offered to split it, unless you know I am not interested in paying my own way. Many serious misunderstandings arise from not knowing where the other person's boundaries are. They are different for different people, and people who tend to have rigid boundaries don't understand this.

In a healthy relationship, partners try to let each other know what their boundaries are. They discuss them before the fact whenever possible, but if not then, later. For example, "I knew you meant well when you cleaned my room, but I felt enraged. That is my space, and although I would prefer it neat, it has to be my problem if it isn't."

A simple act for one person can be a major issue for another. Respecting and understanding boundaries is part of the process of becoming closer.

Boundaries and barriers are different. There is a private space that belongs to me and me alone. It is not that I choose to shut you out. It is, rather, that my space needs to be respected if I am to be fully myself and fully functional.

For many, violation of that space causes irritability and a variety of physical symptoms. I develop symptoms of suffocation if my private space is violated. Others have different reactions. Some have a greater need for space and privacy than others. The issue needs to be talked about in order to be respected and not misunderstood.

Relationship Myth Number 11:

"You will instinctively anticipate my every need, desire and wish."

Relationship Truth Number 11:

In the real world, if needs, desires and wishes are not clearly communicated, it is unlikely they will be fulfilled.

Underlying Issue: Expectations

You have learned in the process of growing up that it is not in your best interest to have expectations. If you have an expectation, you will, at the least, be disappointed or, at most, devastated. It depends on what the promise is and how much it means to you. Unfulfilled promises run all the way from "I'll buy you an ice cream cone" to "I'll send you to college."

You learned that the only way to protect yourself is not to expect anything from anybody. It's a rough way to live, but it's safe. You cut your losses.

But—that ever-present "but"—you also cut your gains.

Healthy relationships involve expectations. Not only do they involve expectations, they involve a shared commitment to fulfill them. The shared part is very important because it means that you have to tell your partner what you want and there is an agreement to attempt to meet your needs. To want flowers for your birthday and then become devastated if you don't get them is not fair to your partner if he had no idea you expected flowers. If he knew and didn't fulfill your expectations, it is important to talk about it because it may be a signal of difficulty in your relationship.

Many people want their partners to please them by being mind readers. That is a setup and comes out of your fears and your questions about whether you are worth anything. If he anticipates your desires when you don't ask, you don't have to suffer over the issue of your value. If he doesn't, and you don't ask, you can then put yourself down and lock in your negative feelings about yourself.

If you decide that you will express your desires and they are fulfilled, that is wonderful. But you will probably find the situation stressful because it is unfamiliar. The body does not differentiate between dis-stress (bad) and eu-stress (good), and you, as a result, may be inclined to sabotage the relationship if it is going too smoothly. That is a response to reduce the stress, but there is the risk that you will once again begin to judge yourself negatively. After all, if you were a good person, you wouldn't do that. Good things take getting used to. Give yourself a break by allowing some time for the adjustment.

If you make your wishes clear and they are not met, it is important to understand what is going on. If the desire seems reasonable to you, and it was not met, you need to find out why. You need to check it out. You may not have been clear. Your partner may not be listening to you. Your partner may be caring about you in terms of himself and not in terms of you. You may have made a demand that he could not fulfill. You might say, "If you care about me and do not express it in ways that are meaningful to me, your caring is not useful to me. It does not enhance me; it only enhances you." Once this is understood, if there is no attempt to accommodate your needs, it is a sign that the relationship is not developing in a healthy way. Either your demands are too great for your partner to meet, or your partner is too self-centered to accommodate you. This is important for you to know regardless of how the relationship is progressing. If you require a lot of nurture, you will not be satisfied in a relationship with someone who is aloof. It simply won't work.

Mutually agreed-upon expectations are essential to a healthy relationship. Explaining away continual disappointment will not get you what you want. People do disappoint those they care about, even in healthy relationships. But it does not happen often.

Harry, an American, married Yael, an Israeli, and the couple came to live in this country. Yael made it very clear to Harry that she needed to return home at least once a year. This was an expectation she had—after all, she was going to leave the land of her birth to make her life with him. Since they knew this from the beginning, they were able to plan for it and it became a part of the way that they lived their lives together.

Sometimes people don't express their desires to spend time with their families and don't set up ground rules for how that can work out and it leads to conflict, the results of which can be serious.

If you grew up in a substance abusing family and attended a support group such as Al-Anon, one of the things that you probably learned was that you could not have expectations of someone who is suffering from the disease of alcoholism. You needed to learn this in order to protect yourself emotionally. This is an emotional pattern that is very helpful to you in that kind of situation. However, the idea in developing a healthy, intimate relationship is to allow yourself to become vulnerable. And one of the ways in which you become vulnerable is to have expectations of each other.

For example, if you were making plans with an alcoholic and he said, "I'll pick you up at 3:00 PM to take you to the store," you would also need to have an alternate plan to protect yourself from the inconsistency. If you are in a healthy relationship and your partner says, "I'll pick you up at 3:00 PM," then you need to be able to assume that he will. And if he doesn't, that is something that you can talk about and resolve so that expectations will be met. Realistic expectations are important in developing a framework for a healthy relationship.

Many of you do not know what a reasonable expectation is. Is it reasonable for me to ask him to come to my door, rather than sit in the car and wait for me to come out? Is it reasonable for me to want him to wear a tie if we go out to dinner? Is it reasonable for me to ask her to share some of the expenses? A typical reaction is: "Since I don't know what a reasonable expectation is, and since I don't want to look like a jerk, perhaps I should just keep my mouth shut and see what happens."

That attitude may have some validity, but it is also a way to avoid confronting an even bigger fear. Confronting the discomfort is a big step toward developing healthy intimacy. Couples develop their own norms and fulfill mutual expectations. But first, the expectations need to be expressed and discussed.

Relationship Myth Number 12:

"If I am not in complete control at all times, there will be anarchy."

Relationship Truth Number 12:

In the real world, one is in charge of one's life and takes control of situations as needed, by conscious decision and agreement. There are also times to share control and times to give up control.

Underlying Issue: Control

"If I am not in control, everything will fall apart." You learned that lesson very early. You controlled your life as best you could because without order there would be anarchy.

What are the implications of this approach to control in a relationship? Healthy relationships are not power struggles. They involve give and take and shared responsibility. They also involve not having to do everything all by yourself.

To you these are just words. "I moved without asking for help from anyone!" Ann says empathically. "Many of my friends offered to help, but I was determined to do it myself. I don't want to owe anybody anything. And nobody would take care of my things the way I do."

Ann feels that if she accepts help, she loses control of her life. Her possessions will be ruined and she will be forever obligated.

There is also the fear of being dependent. "If I let him help me this time and he doesn't disappoint me, when something else comes up I may ask him again, and pretty soon I'll become dependent on him to take care of me. Then I will no longer be able to take care of myself and I'll be stuck." This attitude implies that not being in charge at all times will lead to devastation when the inevitable abandonment occurs.

Ann also does not know how to share: "I know how to do it all," or, "I don't know how to do anything. Balancing responsibility is unfamiliar to me. I don't know how to do it. It may look as if I want to run everything, or as if I run away from doing my part, but it may have to do with not understanding how to work out a balance."

This is something else that needs to be talked about in very specific terms. When your partner says, "It upsets me that every time you say I can do something for you, I know you have a backup in case I let you down." An answer might be, "It has nothing to do with you. I need a little time to accept the idea that I am not in this alone and can give up a little control without being devastated."

An exchange such as this is double-edged because the need for approval and fear of abandonment are so strong in you that you give up emotional control. Children of troubled families fight for situational control but give up their emotional selves. They may declare, "I don't need you." But they don't sleep if they don't hear from you.

This kind of conflict is exhausting and requires a lot of discussion and time to process within the relationship. With work, however, it can be eased.

Relationship Myth Number 13:

"If we really love each other, we will stay together forever."

Relationship Truth Number 13:

In the real world, people stay together and people separate for many reasons. You can love someone and still terminate a relationship.

Underlying Issue: Loyalty

Adult Children are very loyal people and offer loyalty in all relationships. Loyalty, while an integral part of a healthy relationship, has some limitations. Loyalty is best based on a mutual decision about the limits of the relationship. Both parties decide together whether or not they want a monogamous relationship. They discuss the areas in which they feel insecure so that the other person will not carelessly push the wrong button.

For example, if you panic when someone is five minutes late and your partner has no sense of time, an accommodation must be worked out. If both parties respect the needs and wishes of the other, accommodations can be found. "I'll call if I'm running late," or, "give me 15 minutes leeway."

Children of troubled families tend to carry loyalty to an extreme. They remain in relationships they know to be destructive to them. If problems cannot be worked out, it is not a good idea to stay in the continuing fantasy that they can be worked out. That is replaying the childhood wish that life will be wonderful "if only." It didn't work then. It won't work now.

Loyalty in an Adult Child is also a modeled behavior. Couples enmeshed in alcoholism and other debilitating systems do not tend to break up until some semblance of sobriety or order is achieved. They stay together through thin or thinner. As a result, it is easier for you to stay with someone, even after the relationship is no longer working, than to walk away. "How can you be so callous as to hurt another person?" you ask yourself. But you dismiss the ways in which you are being hurt. You invalidate yourself.

Gretchen and Jack had been together for ten years. Neither of them was happy in the relationship. But neither of them considered ending it. When I asked Gretchen why she stayed if all she did was complain, she said, "In my family we don't walk away just because there are problems."

That may be all well and good, but there was no attempt made to resolve the problem. Gretchen had decided she would be loyal to Jack and that's all there was to it. Jack, having grown up in a similar environment, also just accepted that this was the way it was. So they just went on together and were unhappy.

Another aspect of this extreme loyalty comprises a strong desire not to experience the pain of loss. Very often you will have resolved all of the issues involved in ending a relationship that has become toxic. All the air has been taken out of the fantasy balloons on both the intellectual and emotional levels, and yet you do not act: "I'm still stuck! I can't move. What is wrong with me? I'm not afraid of being alone. I know I can manage. Why can't I get unstuck?" Simply stated, you don't want to get unstuck. You *want* to want to get unstuck. As bad as being stuck is, change is worse.

There is no getting around the fact that you will have to go through a mourning period after a relationship ends. Entering into a new relationship immediately only puts it off and interferes with the new relationship. There is no way to avoid experiencing the loss. There is no way to avoid the pain. It is a part of the growth process.

In a relationship, you need to understand and be willing to work on appropriate limits to loyalty. Decide in advance what the limits are and commit yourself to remain aware of them. Recognize when you exceed them and when something else is operating that is not in your best interest. When you start rationalizing, be aware of what you are doing; remember it goes back to your early tapes. But, with work, your attitude can change.

Relationship Myth Number 14:

"My partner will never take me for granted, and always be supportive and non-critical."

Relationship Truth Number 14:

In the real world, things do not always go smoothly, but you always have a right to your feelings.

Underlying Issue: Validation

One of the things you need most is to have your feelings validated. In your alcoholic or dysfunctional family, your feelings were never validated. On the contrary, they were discounted with, "You don't really feel that way. It's not okay to feel that way." So you start feeling peculiar about whether it is okay to feel this way or that way. You need someone who will validate your feelings—not necessarily your behavior, but your feelings.

You need someone to whom you can say, "Gee, that really made me angry. I really wanted to act like that. I really wanted to do this." And you need someone to reply, "I can appreciate those feelings. They are valid." Nobody comes into counseling, nobody goes for help, who has been validated. So it's extremely important, whatever feelings are expressed, for one's partner to validate them: "Sure, you feel that way. Absolutely. That's the way that you feel. You might want to look at it, you might want to feel differently about it. I see it differently, but it's okay to feel however you feel, and it's good for our relationship to let me know what that feeling is. The sharing makes us closer."

The sharing of feelings helps make you closer if you have established a safe climate where sharing feelings is okay. In some circumstances the validation of feelings is critical to the development of a healthy relationship. That is, lack of validation by a partner can get in the way.

A rather extreme example of this occurred recently. A client of mine named Joanie, the daughter of an alcoholic mother, was married to a man who had been in recovery from alcoholism for about eight months. Joanie herself was not an alcoholic, but she was addicted to sugar. Joanie found herself in a difficult time in her life. Her mother was dying of cancer, a long and difficult process. In addition to brain tumors and generalized cancer, Joanie's mother was also suffering from advanced alcoholism. Although Joanie's mother had never consistently served her daughter's needs, Joanie needed to be there for her in order to feel good about herself. If this meant visiting her mother in the hospital every night, or visiting her regularly when she was at home, it was important to Joanie that she do it. For the sake of her own sense of self, she could not walk away from what she considered her responsibility at that time.

Joanie's husband reacted negatively to this situation. Before her mother became ill, she had been a constant thorn in their sides. She had done everything she could to destroy their relationship, and even to destroy her daughter Joanie. Now she was even taking away the precious little time the couple had to spend together.

James became very hostile. "I don't like you going to visit your mother every night," he said. "We never see each other. What kind of relationship do we have!" He became so angry and jealous that it was no exaggeration to say that he was behaving like a selfish little boy.

Joanie's response to James's behavior was very defensive.

"Your attitude really sucks," she said. "My mother will be dead before long, and I need to do this for her. You and I have the rest of our lives to spend together. It is unfair of you to begrudge me this time. Your lack of understanding of my needs is absolutely appalling."

The yelling went back and forth. They were in constant conflict. She felt justified in her position and he felt justified in his. Neither one validated the other's feelings in any way.

The reality here is that they weren't really disagreeing. The situation really was terrible. James' mother-in-law's illness really was taking away the scarce time that James and Joanie had to spend together, and the situation was unfortunate and uncomfortable for all of them. Meanwhile, Joanie was spending a great deal of time with her mother and still not receiving any validation from her mother for all she was doing to care for her. The fact that her mother was dying did not serve any of Joanie's needs. So, once again, Joanie was giving and giving.

It would have been ideal if James had been in the stage of his own development where he could have been supportive of her at this time, but the reality was that he was not able to do so. It also would have been ideal if Joanie had been in a stage of her own recovery where she did not have to devote herself totally to her mother, but she was not. If this couple had been able to validate each other's positions, the friction that existed between them would have virtually disappeared.

Joanie needed to say to her husband, "I agree with you. You are absolutely right. My mother is a pain in the ass. You and I are not spending enough time together, and she is taking away from the precious little time that we have together. Yes, I am resentful that I need to do this for myself and that I haven't reached a point where I can be more reasonable in serving my mother's needs." If she had been able to do this instead of defending her mother and defending her own right to be there for her mother, the two of them would not have been in conflict. She would not have had to behave any differently. She would have been capable of saying, "I wish I were able to be less compulsive about this, and that I could serve both our own needs and my mother's needs. I wish I were further along in my growth."

And once Joanie had validated James' feelings, he would no longer have had to feel as defensive, and then neither would she. He could then have gone on to validate her feelings with something like, "I am glad you understand how I feel. This situation really makes me angry, but I can also understand how there will be no living with you if you do not do what you see as your responsibility right now."

Validation can be the key to getting through a crisis. Without validation it is quite possible that the damage done to the relationship will be irreparable. Without validation Joanie won't be able to forgive James for his "stinking thinking," and he won't be able to forgive her for abandoning him when he wanted and needed her.

This story does have a happy ending. Joanie and James were finally able to validate each other and the pressure on their relationship eased. One afternoon, Joanie happened accidentally to overhear a private conversation between her mother and her mother's nurse. Joanie's mother was telling the nurse how much she loved Joanie, how proud she was of her and how appreciative she was of her daughter's care and attention.

When Joanie told her mother she had overheard the conversation, they cried together and shared the depth of their love. And her mother was then able to die well because she had finally begun to live well.

Validation does not mean agreement. It means respect for similarities and differences. It is the cornerstone of good, solid communication. Without validation, communication is merely a power play.

CHAPTER 4

Issues Of Sexuality

As the social climate changes, the nature of relationships change. If one takes a look at the last forty years, one observes that what has gone on societally in terms of changes in the larger culture has also greatly influenced the sexual behavior between couples.

In the 1950s there was much discussion about whether or not a girl should be a virgin when she married. Many people believed that if you said no you meant maybe, and that if you said maybe you meant yes. And, of course, only the "not nice" girls ever said yes. There was also a lot of discussion over whether sex education should be brought into the schools or stay at home. Alcohol use was rampant to help people "loosen up," but drugs were not even much discussed. There was some debate about marijuana, but it was not an important issue.

By the time we reached the beginning to mid-1960s, all bets were off. Drug use had become rampant, although not necessarily in an addictive way. Everybody was experimenting. And along with that experimentation came a new attitude toward sex. Suddenly sex and relationships did not necessarily have to relate to one another, and all varieties of sexual experimentation blossomed. Needless to say, there was a corresponding rise in venereal disease.

By the 1970s, it was not unusual for people of different sexes to share apartments even if they weren't involved in a romantic or sexual relationship. Neither was it any longer unusual for couples who *were* romantically involved to live together without the benefit of marriage. Parents took a "firm" stand: "They will sleep in separate rooms in my house. Not that I don't care what they do at school, but I can't change what they do at school."

Addiction became a lot more serious and cocaine use became rampant as the 1980s swung into high gear. Meanwhile, the sexual climate became somewhat less frenetic even as more pressure was exerted in the school to teach kids how to prevent pregnancies. Of course by then whether or not they could be taught about reproduction had long ceased to be an issue in all but the most fundamentalist areas of the country.

Toward the end of the 1980s, it became apparent that a new sexually transmitted disease had developed which was fatal, and for which there was no cure. Heterosexuals felt relatively safe when the first outbreaks of the HIV virus were confined mainly to the male homosexual community and to IV drug users.

But in the 1990s, it seems as if once again all bets are off. Couples no longer enter into casual sex, but for their own safety they must discuss issues pertaining to safe sex. This takes a lot of the spontaneity, the going trend in the 1960s and 1970s, out of the relationship. Transmission of the HIV virus has reached epidemic proportions and indeed has changed the way people relate to each other sexually. The homosexual community, first to begin to address the problem in a responsible way, has seen the percentages of infection drop substantially.

However, the incidence of HIV infection in the heterosexual community continues to rise. And the statement, "When I sleep with you,

I also sleep with everyone that you have slept with," takes on a significance that it never had before. The days have passed when a female could take prophylactic precautions against pregnancy and disease even if she was uncomfortable having a discussion with her partner.

So the period of time when there was a more relaxed attitude about sex is gone and sexual practices and mores are now closer to what they were in the 1950s than they have been at any other time since. To put all this in perspective, the point here is that we were all influenced by the times in our sexual attitudes and behaviors. And as times change, to a degree so do we. Essentially we develop our own thoughts and attitudes, but social influence is unavoidable.

None of this negates what I am about to say, but it helps to put the present issue into perspective.

GENERAL ISSUES

What happens to a couple in the sexual part of their relationship is symptomatic of everything else that is happening. The issues presented here show up in other places, as sexual intimacy is one means of communicating and sharing oneself.

The questions I hear are endless: "What's normal? How long does it take to be in 'synch' sexually? Is it a good idea to be honest about sexual experiences and attitudes? Am I any good? Am I good enough? Can sex be fun? Is there a lot to know? How do I keep from holding back? If I'm free, will I be more vulnerable? Am I seen only as a sex object? Do I have to give up control?"

Ask the questions. Read the literature. Talk about sex with your partner. Find out what works for you. The couple decides what is normal for them and it is a shared learning experience. Discuss the things that get in the way. Some are easily resolved, while others that are historically based will take time to overcome. The parental relationship you saw in your childhood was distorted in many ways, including the sex life. It may have influenced you in ways that make your sexual adjustment difficult and leave you with questions about your sexuality. You may be as confused about your sexuality as you are about other aspects of your life.

Celebration of yourself in any aspect of your life is difficult. So you need to take a look at what sex means to you. Joseph said, "My parents fought. Then they had sex and everything was fine. I always understood sex was a way to end an argument, but I knew there had to be something wrong with that." The missing piece is that there was no resolution of the conflict. Sex was used as a way to avoid problem-solving rather than to enhance the relationship.

Here is another example: "My mother told me having sex was a woman's duty. It wasn't pleasurable, but it put men to sleep. I don't want that for myself, but I feel guilty if I don't perform when asked."

To resolve these feelings, a couple should talk about their sexual relationship, especially their expectations.

Again, "Sex was always a control and power issue in my house. It was linked to physical abuse. I am so afraid it will happen to me that I remain celibate."

This is a deep and serious problem that needs to be worked out with a therapist. A caring partner can help, but more is probably necessary in a case like this.

Many men and women have reported an inability to climax. When explored, it becomes clear that there is a holding back in other areas of the relationship as well. It is a fear of being vulnerable, because being vulnerable has always meant pain. It is a very clear demonstration of how the lack of risk-taking can limit an experience.

Alcoholism results in even more complex problems. Martha related the following: "My father cheated on my mother, and my two alcoholic husbands cheated on me. As a result, I don't want to get sexually involved with anyone because I don't think I could go through that again. I think that's probably one of the reasons why I have gained all of this weight."

A discussion of alcoholics, and the need for alcoholics to have enablers, will not work with this lady. She has decided on a deep level that it is her own lack of desirability that caused her husbands to be unfaithful. Somehow she also finds herself responsible for her father's philandering. Putting on a lot of weight is a way to avoid the issue: if no one finds her sexually desirable, then she does not have to deal with the issue. Fortunately, she is working with a good therapist who will help her discover her sexual self and recognize that the difficulty lies not in her lack of desirability, but in her selection of a partner. As she changes and grows, her choices will be more compatible with who she really is.

In healthy relationships, decisions about monogamy evolve as the relationship progresses. When people are first getting to know each other, it is not unusual for them to be involved with others too. As the relationship develops, they make decisions about exclusivity. When alcoholism is involved, the rules get shifted. Early on there is monogamy, but as the disease progresses it is not unusual for the alcoholic to seek out other partners. Other folks may tend to look for comfort outside the marriage as well. Another problem I hear is, "The only place that I feel powerful and in control is in the bedroom. I begin to believe that that is the only thing that I have to offer another person. It makes me very sad." Take heart If you are capable of being a good partner in the bedroom, you are capable of being a good partner in other aspects of the relationship. What goes on in the bedroom generalizes to other places.

Being technically good is something else again. If you are merely technically good, we are not talking about a relationship. In a relationship, emotional investment and caring are primary. You have probably not given yourself enough credit for being able to express your feelings. The bedroom may be a place where you can do that. Somehow you have used your freedom in this area as another means of beating yourself rather than using it to celebrate yourself.

The opposite is also true: "I love my husband very much," said Lynn. "He is very dear to me, and we are good friends as well as being husband and wife. I want to share my entire life with him, but I don't want to make love to him. In my house, lovemaking was like violation. I am terrified that this is what it will evolve into."

When I talked to Lynn about lovemaking, it became clear that she was actually talking about intercourse. When I asked her if she enjoyed having her husband say affectionate things to her, or having him put his arms around her, she said, "Oh, yes." When I asked her if they ever just held hands when they went for a walk, she said she enjoyed that too.

The reality here is that Lynn and her husband make love in a variety of ways. Because of her childhood experience, she mistakenly equated intercourse with lovemaking and was not able to see the larger picture. As she became aware of the many aspects of lovemaking that she shared with her husband, she was free from the notion that she would repeat her parents' negative relationship.

The variations on these themes are endless. The underlying problem is, "I am afraid of being close." As you work out other aspects of allowing yourself to be close, the sexual part will work out too. If you find that this area still presents difficulties, it may be time to work with a professional who can help you overcome them. Sex is only one aspect of a relationship, yet the shared closeness can be very important and very significant. Overcoming the distortions resulting from your childhood is important to your personal growth. Remember here, too, you do not have enough information to answer all of your questions. This is probably a large part of what is getting in your way.

Take it easy on yourself. Take it easy on your partner. Once again, the message is: go slowly. In fact, no aspect of a healthy relationship happens overnight. The potential may be immediately obvious, but a relationship is a day-to-day developing experience.

Same-Sex Relationships

Adult Children's concerns about having healthy, intimate relationships are the same in same-sex relationships as those in opposite sex relationships. These concerns, however, are compounded because of the difficulties involved in being homosexual in a culture that is largely homophobic. Though the issues are the same for those involved in same-sex relationships, they are exaggerated by the larger culture. The ability to share oneself openly, honestly and freely without fear of the consequences is impaired by living in a troubled home. Learned defensive behaviors have to be turned around in order to have a healthy relationship, especially for the homosexual whose need for defenses has been reinforced in the mainstream.

Clients I see who are involved in same-sex relationships fall roughly into three categories. First, there are those who have been aware of their sex preference for as long as they can remember and have spent time and energy dealing with, and coming to grips with, what that reality means to them. For these people, the struggle is the same as for those involved in opposite sex relationships, except that the struggle may be more pronounced.

The second group consists of those who are just becoming aware of their sexuality. They are people of all ages who have just admitted on a conscious level that they have a same-sex preference. Many of the symptoms they have carried with them during their lives begin to disappear. One symptom is depression, which begins to abate for many once they have acknowledged their sex preference. This group is very similar to the blossoming adolescent who is becoming aware of herself as a sexual being for the first time and is excited about it, afraid of it and has to test it out by going through many experiences to find out how things work. This person experiences the great joy and great pain of the adolescent extremes. The age may seem inappropriate, but one must go through all of these stages regardless of when the awareness hits. An additional complication may arise from the fact that many of these people are married, have children and have complicated lives in the heterosexual world. They need to make decisions as to the best way to handle the rest of their lives.

The third group consists of those who have decided that because they have had such horrendous relationships with the opposite sex, starting invariably with the parent of the opposite sex, they do not want to repeat the experience. As a result, they decide they will become involved only in same-sex relationships. Needless to say, this does not work. Whether or not an individual has or does not have a penis does not mean that the individual will have the same personality type as those you have been involved with before, or as your mother or father. It has been my experience that people who run to same-sex relationships as a way of avoiding repetition of the horrors of the past run the risk of picking the same personality type they picked in heterosexual relationships.

The important consideration here is that they come to grips with the underlying issues from which they are fleeing. A healthy choice of partner is possible, regardless of sex.

The essentials for intimacy for lesbians and gay men who are children of troubled families are no different from those in opposite sex relationships. The difficulties are compounded by society, but the struggle is the same.

INCEST

Although incest is not necessarily part of all troubled family systems, it is present frequently enough to warrant discussion.

Incest is a much more widespread manifestation of dysfunction in families than we have yet begun to explore. The family system where alcoholism is present, for example, is fertile ground for it to occur. There is no doubt that those of you who are survivors of incest have an additional dimension of great difficulty in establishing healthy, intimate relationships.

Although incest occurs between mothers and sons, fathers and sons, and among siblings, the most common form is between fathers and daughters. The last will therefore be the focus of discussion here.

Incest can be overt or covert. Overt incest is defined as sexual contact within the family. Though not necessarily actual intercourse, it involves sexual contact in one form or another. The most usual forms involve fondling of breasts and genitals, use of the child to masturbate, and oral sex. Covert incest involves many of the same dynamics, but there is no actual physical contact.

Some of the considerations present include the taboo against talking about what is going on and the isolation of the family. In many incestuous families, one of the daughters, usually the oldest, has taken over many of the responsibilities of running the household and looking after the younger children. Fulfilling her father sexually may be looked upon as an extension of the role of "little mother." There is a greater likelihood that this behavior will occur if there is a role reversal between mother and daughter. This role reversal happens often when the mother is chronically ill or alcoholic.

How does incest relate to later intimate relationships? First, the ability to trust, which has been discussed earlier, is destroyed. The most outrageous aspect of an incestuous relationship precludes a "safe harbor." The child has no one to run to.

I have asked many clients who were incest survivors why they didn't tell someone: "Why did you wait until your late twenties or early thirties to let someone know that you were abused as a child?"

Invariably, the response is, "What good would it have done? If I had told my mother, it would have made no difference. She would not have believed me, or dealt with it. It would only have made circumstances worse. I certainly could not have gone to anyone outside the family." These children had no place to turn, no one to help them.

So here is a circumstance where you found out at a very early age that there was no one to trust. You certainly could not trust the parent who was sexually abusing you, nor the other parent. So you learned that the only one you could trust was yourself. Because of this early, and generally continuing, experience what you learned is quite clear. First, you learned that you cannot trust because if you do, you will be hurt. Moreover, you learned that there is no one to trust. This early experience greatly exaggerates the difficulty you have later on in trusting someone in an intimate relationship.

Second, incest affects your present sexual behavior. It is not unusual for incest survivors in a sexual relationship with another person to flashback on the horrors of their childhood. They will flashback while in a loving relationship to the experiences of childhood and this causes problems.

Third, some survivors of incest believe they can only obtain love and affection through sex. If the sexual experience with the father was pleasurable, they see themselves as having tremendous sexual powers. This fantasy distorts the development of a healthy, intimate relationship. It also leads to idealizing men.

Fourth, many decide to involve themselves in same-sex relationships because they never again want to face the dreaded penis. However, the other distortions and difficulties continue to come into play. The difficulty of trusting does not go away because you are involved in a same-sex relationship. Neither parent could be trusted. So this, in and of itself, is not a solution to the problem.

When incest is covert rather than overt, some of the same circumstances apply. The father treats the little girls like his wife or his love object. He is jealous of her suitors and makes subtle sexual innuendoes. She does many of the things that in other circumstances his wife might do. The result here is somewhat different. The child doesn't feel abused: she feels idealized. She also idealizes the parent, which makes it extremely difficult for her to relate to other men. Because her daddy is the perfect love object, she seeks out men who are like her father in an attempt to replace him.

This is a very difficult bond to break. How can you want to pull away from someone who makes you feel so special? How can you find someone else who will adore you unconditionally? The pain of working this through is excruciating. Although your sexual fantasies have not been experienced in the real world, they may be powerful enough to keep you from appreciating someone else. It is a mistake to underestimate the hold of a covertly incestuous relationship.

The child's reaction to the violation of incest is on a very deep level and must be addressed on that level. With most issues concerned with living in an alcoholic home, the mere flushing them out by discussion with people who understand, who have had the same experiences, goes a long way toward resolving them.

This is not usually the case with incest, so it is very important to work this out with a professional. You must come to grips with the guilt and shame that incest survivors feel. Somehow there is always the sense that: "I am responsible." "Why does it happen to me and not to my sister?" Or, "If it happened to both my sister and me, why didn't I do anything to prevent it?" Since children are compliant for the most part, when they reflect back they see themselves as going along with it, as being willing, as not fighting against incest. They feel responsibility, which is neither valid nor true.

Today you would not permit this kind of behavior, but the adult you are now did not exist when you were a child. Take a look at yourself as a small child and tell her she is guilty for what happened. It is not possible for her to be guilty for this! Relieving the guilt, however, is not as easy as intellectually understanding that you could not have been responsible. Many who have taken over the role of the mother even feel that the incestuous experience protected the mother. This is similar to a child taking a beating for other siblings, or the mother, so the others will not have to endure it.

At any rate, you were not responsible. The guilt you feel because you were powerless to stop incest from happening is inappropriate. You had no choice because you knew no alternatives.

The shame you feel is also inappropriate. The sense of yourself as a disgusting person, as someone who experienced incest because you were disgusting, is not true. You were not disgusting. You were a victim, and you were trapped. You need to work out these feelings of shame in order to feel good about yourself. Otherwise your shame will get in the way of developing a healthy sexual relationship, where you can celebrate your body as wholesome and good.

Do not try to do this alone. Today there are many therapists who specialize in working with incest survivors. It is important to work with someone who is not only sensitive to your type of family system, but sensitive to what happens to children who have been sexually abused. I cannot emphasize this strongly enough because the pathology of sexual abuse is deeper than the results of alcoholism. I am not, however, minimizing the pain and struggle that one has for the rest of one's life as a result of living in an alcoholic home.

You are not alone. You will be flabbergasted, once you begin to share your experience, at how many others have also been through it. Just as keeping the secret of living with alcoholism or other trouble was not to your advantage, keeping the secret of incest also works against you. Sharing this secret can be the start of setting you free. It is in no way a reflection on you that you had a parent who was sick enough to use you in this way.

For more detail I suggest you read my book, *Healing Your Sexual Self.* There is an important chapter in that book that deals with how the partner can be helpful in doing his or her share to make the relationship work.

CHAPTER 5

So You Love An Adult Child

In the years since this book was first published, I have received many letters and phone calls from people who have been involved with Adult Children. The predominant theme has been that just as soon as they felt the relationship was going well, the other person panicked and ended the involvement. The partner is left feeling frantic and confused. She simply doesn't know what to do, and the reality is that what happened really has very little to do with her. For many Adult Children, the betrayal in childhood was by the person they trusted the most. As a result, when the level of trust is built and real intimacy begins to develop, a red flag goes up emotionally and the person cannot tolerate the relationship as the early fear of betrayal surfaces and becomes unmanageable. As a result, many flee, leaving a shell-shocked partner in their wake.

A woman in exactly this situation called me recently. She had been in a long distance relationship for six years and everything was going wonderfully. Yet as soon as the decision was finally made for her to move to the city where he lived and to normalize the relationship, he abruptly and precipitously cut off the involvement.

"It's not you, it's me," he told her. "I don't know what it is, but I know I have to be by myself."

"I invested six years of my life in this," she told me. "Are you just going to walk away?"

Unfortunately, in this situation, the answer was yes. There are no choices here. If he had left because of her, there may have been things she could do to retrieve the relationship. But he left because of him and because of his response to early childhood triggers, And she has to respect that.

With help, change is possible. Without help, individuals will go from relationship to relationship because just at the point in each relationship where a commitment needs to be made, they will choose to end the relationship instead.

The reason this relationship worked until she wanted to normalize it by moving to the city where her partner lived is that for an Adult Child, being in harmony with the person one trusts the most just isn't "normal." The early childhood template of betrayal and chaos that informs an Adult Child's emotional behavior says that rejection and trauma are passionate and trust and acceptance simply are not. So if she does not duplicate the behaviors of the rejecting parent, he is stymied.

This is the bad news. On the other hand, it is not at all surprising to me that you have fallen in love with an Adult Child. Children of alcoholics are the most loving and loyal people around. They offer more than any other group of people I know. I am certain that you, too, are impressed at what they are able to offer in a relationship, or you would not be involved with one.

And even though you may not have experienced exactly the same situation as the woman who sadly had to cancel her plans to move to

Pittsburgh, I am sure that at times your relationship with an Adult Child is very confusing to you, too.

Just when you think everything is fine, just when you think that the relationship is the most fantastic, beautiful, intense, intimate, exciting experience of your life, your Adult Child backs off. You don't know what hit you. Just when you think you have a thorough understanding, he or she does something contrary. Many times your Adult Child will react in ways that seem peculiar to you, in ways that make absolutely no sense. Naturally, you will find yourself confused. This chapter is designed to help you better understand what goes on in your partner's mind. More often than not, your partner's peculiar behavior has nothing to do with you, although your behavior may trigger it. And often if you can recognize this and respond accordingly, the two of you will be able to work through the problem together.

I do not suggest that you behave any differently than you do now unless it is useful for both you and your partner for mutual behaviors to be modified. The discussion that follows is designed to let you know what is going on so that your reactions in a given situation will be more responsive to what is really happening to your Adult Child.

Understanding what makes your partner tick will be very useful to you and to your relationship. When Adult Children respond peculiarly to situations, it is often because they do not know how to react differently. They do not know that there are other options and they do not know what is appropriate. Many times I hear, "How could I do the right thing if I don't know what right is?" It may be that there are no "rights." But there are certainly responses which are appropriate.

For example, people who have typical backgrounds can more easily confront others than those who come from alcoholic homes. If you are in a restaurant, and the person at the next table is smoking, which is offensive to you, it is natural to ask him to put out the cigarette or blow the smoke in another direction. Your Adult Child, on the other hand, may start squirming in the chair, or become terrified. Your Adult Child has many feelings that would never occur to you. Depending on the history, there might be a great deal of fear, along with a sense of protection, toward you and an overwhelming sense of gratitude to you for taking care of the situation.

Confrontation is never easy for children of alcoholics. And it is especially difficult for them to confront you in an intimate relationship. It is also not easy for them to observe you confronting someone else, regardless of how insignificant the confrontation is. I am not saying don't do it. Simply be aware of the possibility that the reaction may be something different from what you anticipate.

Several bottom line fears children of alcoholics have will affect their responses to you. Your understanding can help alleviate them. I am not suggesting that all Adult Children have all of these fears, but they probably have one or more of them:

Fear Number 1: "I am afraid that I will hurt you."

This fear results from the fact that Adult Children are not taught how to speak and behave appropriately. The behaviors they develop result from watching others. Although many of them do behave appropriately, and many are very clever, charming and articulate, they don't really believe they are. They are afraid they will violate your boundaries. They are afraid that, without meaning to, they will say something or behave in a way that will be hurtful to you. If they do these things, it is not deliberate but because they don't know there are alternatives. As a result, Adult Children tend not to be spontaneous, and you may frequently sense that they are holding back. This is something worth checking out. You might say to the Adult Child you are involved with, "Let's take the risk. If you do or say something that hurts me, I will tell you, just as I want you to tell me if I do something that hurts you. This is the only way we can really get to know each other and be attentive to each other's feelings."

Fear Number 2: "The person you see does not exist."

Children of Alcoholics are so concerned with trying to look and behave normally that in many ways they fabricate the person they would like to be, or the kind of person they think you would like them to be. Chances are this mask does not work as well as they think it does. You are probably able to see who he or she really is, and that is who you are attracted to. This is difficult for the Adult Child to believe. The outside looks good. While outside behavior is exciting and interesting, however, inside there is fear and trembling. Although both parts of the person are valid and true, the Adult Child feels that the outer side that looks confident is not real, and the inner self that is frightened is the real self. Therefore, you have been fooled into believing the inner self does not exist. Ideally, it would be good for the Adult Child to express his or her fears and have self-confidence. Though both parts of the person exist, the Adult Child is not sure you see her as she really is. Worse yet, if you did, you would no longer find her interesting and attractive. The desirable, interesting, attractive, intelligent, charming, sexual person with whom you believe you are involved does not really exist in her mind.

Fear Number 3: "I'll lose control of my life."

My mother was out of control; my father was out of control; and they were in control of me. What a terrible thought! What a horrible memory! I cannot let it happen again. Since I am so unsure of myself, I am afraid that if I get close to you, I will defer to you in all things. I will let you make all the decisions because I am afraid I will make the wrong ones. I really don't want to do that, but I am uncertain I will be strong enough not to give in. Therefore, I will back away from you or make preposterous demands that you cannot possibly fulfill in order to prove to myself that you want control.

To counteract this problem, you have to sit down as a couple and work on decision-making. Adult Children do not have a strong sense of what alternatives and consequences are. Discuss the options involved and come to some mutual agreements. Your impatience at indecision, although certainly understandable, will not help your partner make a decision. You may have to allow time to work things through together and to find out if the Adult Child has all of the information necessary to make the decision. You might need to say to your partner, "I am making this decision because there is a time limit. However, that does not mean I am trying to control our relationship. It means only that a decision has to be made." Things that are shared up front are less frightening and can be viewed more realistically.

Fear Number 4: "It doesn't matter anyway."

This is a very defensive position. It comes from a depressed attitude learned in the alcoholic family system, which develops into a depressed lifestyle. When one is depressed, one feels that nothing really matters. This attitude is also somewhat protective: "If I decide that it doesn't matter anyway, then I will be less hurt if something goes wrong. If I allow it to matter, then I will be devastated if something goes wrong." It is also a way of testing. An Adult Child who has this attitude will test you repeatedly to be sure that you will not leave. You may have to confront your partner, saying, "This is a game. I care about you. You do not have to continue to test me." If you don't say anything, and the testing continues, eventually you will leave; you won't be able to handle it.

The testing, however, is not selfishness or wanting to put you through your paces. It comes from insecurity and a rather poor self-image, which only time can cure. Gradually, the defenses will ease up. "It doesn't matter" is akin to "I don't exist," and "If I am not around, you will forget all about me." This is a setup for you to continue to prove that you care. Once you see it as such, you might ask, "How many times do I have to tell you? How much more do I need to show you?"

Fear Number 5: "It's not real."

Your Adult Child may have said to you on many occasions, "This is not real. This is not really happening." She makes these statements when things are going well—when the relationship you share is something that you find so wonderful and so fine and so rare that you can hardly believe it. For you, not believing it involves real excitement and a sense of incredulousness: "How lucky I am to have found this person with whom I can share and experience so much!" That's probably what you mean when you say, "This is not really happening to me. How fortunate I am!"

When your Adult Child says, "This is not real," it means something different. For many Adult Children, growing up was so traumatic that constant trauma is the only reality they know. When life is going well, the circumstances are so unfamiliar they have a sense of unreality about them. So the effect is unsettling.

When you are walking on clouds and believe that your partner is right there beside you, she may do something to sabotage the relationship. All of a sudden, out of the blue, your Adult Child will pick a fight with you or not answer your phone calls. This kind of thing makes absolutely no sense to you, and you feel pushed away. If things are that wonderful, they cannot be real, so the Adult Child, in order to make them real, will use sabotage.

Since you now know this, you can feel a little less punched in the stomach. You can recognize that an unpleasant reaction does not have to do with you, but with the Adult Child's learned responses. You might simply say, "I have not done anything. Things are good. Just try to relax and go slowly." If your Adult Child runs away, chances are she will be back. You will probably need to do something in order to protect yourself, but realize that the rejection is only temporary. Your understanding will help keep the situation from getting more complicated.

When Adult Children realize what they have done, they feel very guilty and remorseful and decide that you couldn't continue to love them anyway because they are terrible people. If they weren't so terrible, they could enjoy things going well and wouldn't get in the way of their own happiness, etc. If you just roll with it, chances are you can ride this one out too.

Fear Number 6: "You'll see how angry I am."

Adult Children learn to repress their anger. They learn as children that if they express anger like other kids do, it will only create more difficulty. As a result, many are filled with unresolved anger. There is a real fear that the anger felt toward their parents and their backgrounds will leak out in a relationship. They are afraid that their anger will be directed at you in inappropriate ways. They are also afraid that if you see the extent of their anger, it will frighten you away. This may or may not be true, according to your own reactions to anger, and according to what degree you are concerned about other people's reactions to you.

Things happen in a relationship that will trigger early experiences. It is important for you and your Adult Child to know each other well. Then, when something happens that you don't understand on the face of it, you will realize that it relates back to childhood. When your Adult Child reacts with inappropriate anger to a situation, chances are that the degree of anger does not relate to what is going on at the moment.

Sarah asked Tommy if he would move some branches that had fallen off her tree from her front yard to her back yard. They were too heavy for her to carry, and it was not difficult for him. He said he would be very happy to do it for her. When she returned from work and saw that it had not been done, she went into a rage. He was flabbergasted at how angry she was, but said, "I'm sorry. I forgot all about it, but I will get it done for you." It is clear that since she was ready to end the relationship over such a minor thing, she was overreacting. But, if you look at Sarah's reaction in the context of her being an Adult Child, the incident has a great deal of meaning.

First, it was a struggle to ask him to do her a favor. It was very hard for her to say, "I need help with the work." She had learned not to ask for favors because they were never granted. But since she is working on this important relationship, she made a conscious decision to ask.

She is also overly concerned about what her neighbors will think if her yard is messy. This consciousness of other people's opinion of her indicates she is not yet secure with her opinion of herself. When Tommy forgot, she felt completely invalidated by him. Her reasoning goes like this: If he really cared about me, he would recognize that I would not ask him to do anything that was not important to me, and he would not forget. Forgetting to remove the wood means that he does not care about me. Forgetting to remove the wood means that I am not as important to him as he pretends I am.

Certainly, the extent of her anger at him is inappropriate. There is cause for annoyance, but not for the rage that she feels. He was insensitive to her needs in taking her request so casually. He was responding to his own history in the fact that he procrastinates.

This couple needs to discuss this incident thoroughly in order for the relationship to remain healthy. She needs to understand that every request will not be responded to automatically, even though it is difficult for her to ask for help. She also needs to understand that his procrastination is not a reflection of his feelings for her. If his behavior continues, and it is something that she cannot live with, then she may need to reassess the relationship; but, on the face of it, her reaction seems more powerful than the circumstance called for.

Tommy will have to learn that if he agrees to do something, he must do it on the terms of the person who asked him to do it. If he tells her, "Yes, I will do it for you," and understands her urgency, then it is unfair of him not to fulfill the request as it is asked. If he is not certain that he can do what is asked immediately, it is important for him to say, "I will do it for you, but I cannot promise that I will do it right now."

Communication and discussion of feelings are critical for Adult Children and the people with whom they are involved. It is the only way to have a healthy relationship.

Fear Number 7: "I am ashamed of who I am."

You may be shocked when you become aware of how low an opinion the Adult Child with whom you are involved has of herself. It may be nearly impossible for you to understand how this bright, charming, capable, lovable person can see herself as such a JERK! Though it makes no sense to you at all, it is real. And a deep, dark secret.

The reason for this level of shame is that many Adult Children believe they were responsible for the dysfunction in their families. Many were told from the beginning, "Life was great until you came along"; "If you weren't such a brat, I wouldn't be drinking." Not only did many believe that they were responsible for the alcoholism, but as they grew older and understood that alcoholism was a disease, they became disgusted with themselves because they were still angry with their parents and humiliated by their behavior.

The message they gave themselves was, "I must be a very disgusting person if I feel this way about a person who is sick."

It may be that your Adult Child has not invited you to meet her family and you wonder why. This could be part of the reason. Your

Adult Child might be humiliated, while also judging herself for feel-ing this way. At the same time, she is very concerned about what you think—whether you will continue to care if you know what the family situation is like. Although these feelings of responsibility and shame are inappropriate, that does not mean they don't exist. This lovely adult whom you have come to know and care about is still beating herself for childhood experiences over which she had no control. The discovery of this secret causes fear in Adult Children. Once the secret is out in the open, it may lose some power. But the attitude is so deeply rooted, it perpetuates a sense of, "If you really knew me, you wouldn't want to have anything to do with me."

Fear Number 8: "You will get to know me and find out that I am not lovable."

This fear is closely allied to shame. The feeling of not being lovable was learned in early childhood.

The child wanted to find a way to make things okay, to fix them. No matter what she did, it was not good enough. No matter how hard she tried, it did not matter. The child, a powerless victim of the situation, believed that there was something wrong with her because she could not find a way to fix it. If she were truly lovable, she would find a way to make life fine and happy once again.

Many Adult Children have cried in my arms: "I tried to stop it, I tried to make it different, but I just couldn't. And the worst thing of all is that sometimes when my parents were fighting, I didn't even get in the middle of it because I was terrified that I would be next. How could I be lovable if I was thinking about myself first?"

The truth is that the person you care about is lovable. It will be hard for her to accept that. You will need to be patient. It takes time for a self-perception to change.

Fear Number 9: "I want to be comfortable."

The person you care about may back away from an involvement with you by using the argument, "I want to be comfortable." This may make absolutely no sense. The rationale goes something like this: "My whole life has been one series of emotional crises after another. I'm tired of it. I don't want it. I don't want to feel any more. Feelings are very disruptive to me. If I get involved with you, I'm bound to feel. I'm bound to feel ups and downs, and right now I have my whole life in order and don't want to risk screwing it up. Getting involved with you would not allow me to maintain the even keel I'm on now. I will begin to care, and then I'll feel upset. I'll begin to feel a whole variety of things. I don't want that right now! I want to feel comfortable."

This attitude won't last long. It is a fantasy that many Adult Children have when they go through a level period. It won't last, not only because they are active, vibrant people, but because they have no frame of reference for it.

Being comfortable will become extremely boring, and they cannot sustain it. The reality is that the development of a healthy relationship will afford them a level of comfort that has not been experienced before. But that is a long process, requiring much hard work.

Fear Number 10: "You'll leave me anyway."

Your Adult Child may be afraid to get involved because of fear of abandonment. The fear that the person with whom she is involved will walk out on her is absolutely terrifying. This fear is different from the fear of rejection. Fear of abandonment is much deeper: "If you abandon me, and I am left all by myself, I will die."

This, too, has its roots in childhood, and not in the real world. It results in an initial fear of getting involved at all. But once the decision is made to become involved, you may find that your Adult Child is very possessive, jealous and insecure where you are concerned. This disconcerting behavior comes from fear of abandonment. It is a big problem because if this possessiveness gets out of hand, you may be forced to do exactly what your partner fears the most. It is therefore important for you to continue to reassure your Adult Child that you do care, that you are not going to leave, but that it's important for you to have other people in your life. It is also important for your partner to have other people in her life. Rather than harming a relationship, other friends enhance it. You may need to reinforce this idea many, many times, at the same time being aware that the possessiveness comes from a very basic fear of abandonment.

You also need to be careful not to disappoint your partner. Other people react much more casually when you forget to call or are an hour late. But Adult Children tend to overreact to this kind of behavior; they begin to panic. You need to understand this so your relationship can develop, flourish and provide the security necessary to both of you.

You may be wondering at this point whether or not it's worth struggling with all the fears I have outlined. Try to bear a few things in mind. First, not all Adult Children suffer from all of these fears. Second, not all people are free from these fears, even though they did not grow up in a troubled family. Third, Adult Children have great difficulties in their relationships with themselves. Their greatest difficulty is the lack of ability to experience themselves as valuable and worthy and lovable. Their greatest asset is their ability to offer you the sense that you are valuable and worthy and lovable. There is much to be gained from being involved with an Adult Child. The difficulties you face can be overcome if both members of the partnership are willing to work on them. With awareness and understanding come the potential for resolution of most difficulties.

Knowing the characteristics shared by many Adult Children can help give a direction to effect change. Being able to pinpoint areas of difficulty makes it easier to offer opinions for making the struggle for a healthier relationship that much easier.

CHAPTER 6

Now That You're Ready To Create A Healthy Relationship

So now that you know what a healthy relationship is, just how exactly do you go about creating one?

You have to start by making sure that the two of you are in the same relationship.

This may sound rather obvious. But if you come from a family where thoughts and feelings were not exchanged, you will tend not to share your own thoughts and feelings and make assumptions about how others think and feel. As a result, you will fantasize what someone else is thinking and feeling, and invariably end up disappointed when that person doesn't react in the way that you had hoped.

You sit home waiting for the phone to ring, sure that he doesn't care because he doesn't call every night. If you asked him why, he might just tell you that he spends the whole working day on the phone so he really hates making calls at night. But if you'd be willing to call him he'd love to talk to you.

I once asked a client of mine who was engaged to be married what she wanted in a husband. She wrote me pages and pages and pages about who her ideal husband would be. She knew exactly how he would treat her, how he would treat her children, what kind of family he had, his feelings about household responsibilities, religion and almost every other detail of how their lives would unfold together.

But when I asked her which of these qualities her fiancé had, she replied, "None of them."

It turned out that they had absolutely nothing in common except that they had met at a mixer for divorced Catholics. Eventually, and at great emotional expense to both of them, the engagement was broken off.

So if you're looking toward a healthy, long-term relationship with an eye on living together or getting married, there are a number of things that you have to know about yourself and the other person before you decide to take that step. The two of you don't have to agree totally on everything. However, you do have to be aware of the many differences that exist between the two of you and how important each difference is to each of you.

Just because you're attracted to someone and enjoy spending time with that person doesn't automatically mean that everything else about a relationship will work out. It may mean that. But until you find out whether you're in the same relationship, you won't know one way or the other. So there are many questions you need to answer.

In no particular order, here are topics you need to explore, both for yourself and with the other person, before you can get an idea of whether the two of you may have a long-term future:

1. Do you and your partner have similar sexual appetites?

Some people enjoy the physical expression of their relationship more than others. After the initial passionate stages have passed and the relationship starts to normalize, a difference like this can become a problematic area. And certainly in this day and age discussions concerning prophylactics have to occur, whereas twenty or thirty years ago the subject could be avoided. If tastes and needs are different, both of these are potential causes of conflict. When you are considering a long-term involvement, further discussion is warranted.

2. How will finances be handled?

Who is in charge of paying bills? What decisions are made about household repairs? The way a couple manages their money is symptomatic of everything else that goes on in their relationship. If you have been on your own, then the idea of pooling finances with someone else can cause a great deal of anxiety. Making joint decisions about how to spend money can be just as challenging.

Therefore, you and your prospective partner need either to share the same values as far as spending money is concerned or to have a major discussion about the places where the two of you differ. How does he feel if you keep a separate bank account? Or how does she feel if you have one? Ideally, what kind of expenditures would each of you consult with the other about before incurring? How do the two of you feel about credit and risk-taking?

You may know some or all of these answers from the experience you already have together, but the only way you can get credit for them in Dr. Jan's book is if you've had the discussion. This way, when one of you later comes to feel differently and says, "I never said that," your partner will be able to point out that yes, indeed you did. People do change. But you need to start with a baseline understanding because basic attitudes don't change. "When we were courting, you bought me beautiful, expensive presents and we went to lovely restaurants. Now you only want to go to McDonald's. What happened? Have the rules changed because we've made a commitment and now you take me for granted?" You don't have to have a whole contract written out between the two of you, all you need is that basic baseline understanding. So if you're used to buying clothes and not looking at the price tags, be sure either that the person you become seriously involved with can go along with that or that you are willing to refocus the habit.

3. How much do you like to socialize?

Do you both like to go out? Or do you prefer to have people come over? Do you like to go to the movies, the theater, museums? Do you go out for dinner and dancing every Saturday?

You may already know the answers to these questions from courting, but when your relationship becomes permanent, things may change: do you really want to spend time with her personal friends or your personal friends as a couple? And how do you feel about individual nights out for each of you? Would it trouble you if she spends a night a week with the girls, or if every Saturday he plays golf? Would you like to go out for dinner and dancing every weekend, or are you actually looking forward to the moment when you can stay home and rent an old movie as your relationship becomes more permanent? Does the other person know?

Some people have one set of social expectations for a courtship and another, completely different set of expectations for a marriage. Find out whether the person with whom you are seriously involved is one of them.

4. If you have children previous to the relationship, what role do you want the other person to play in your children's lives?

You must be very clear about this one. I know a woman who fantasized that when her fiance became her new husband, he would go out of his way to enrich their lives together in many different ways. She imagined that he would spend time with the kids individually and together, that he would listen to them, guide them, laugh with them, play with them, have occasional dinners alone with them. He would also spend some private time after dinner and before bedtime making sure they did their chores, include them in vacations, pick them up from Scouts and ball games, eat out with them and go to the movies with them.

However, she never discussed any of this with him. And once they were married she discovered he had absolutely no intention of being involved with her kids in anything other than a tangential way. Yes, he was willing to live under the same roof with them, but he made it clear that he was not their father—he was their mother's husband.

5. Where are the two of you spiritually, particularly in terms of organized religion?

Are religious rituals important to you? Do you go to church on Sunday or synagogue on Friday nights? Is this something you would want a partner to do with you? If your partner has religious ideas and beliefs that are different from yours, will these cause conflicts between you? If so, will you be able to live with them?

As people grow older, organized religion tends to become more important to them. So even if you're younger, keep this question in mind. The solution that runs along the lines of, "If we have kids, they'll make the decision for themselves," is a cop-out. Children need to be brought up one way or another. They cannot make an educated choice without a consistent form of exposure. If you choose to have children or already have them, part of your responsibility as a parent is to give them a consistent religious framework that they can either accept or reject.

You absolutely can give children more than one religion, but the two of you have to decide consciously and agree on what ways you will give them both without being counterproductive. For instance, you can give them the celebration of both Christmas and Chanukah. But things get a little trickier when you try to impart both the sense that Jesus is the Messiah and the idea that the Messiah has not yet come. So when it comes to actual religious training as opposed to customs and celebrations, a decision will have to be made.

6. To what degree are you willing to be involved with each other's families?

Will you get together every Sunday with one or the other in-law, and if so will this become a source of contention between you? When you get seriously involved with someone, in a sense you are involved with his or her whole family, so these parameters need to be discussed.

Exactly what level of family involvement will be expected of you? Is it assumed that you will prepare and host complicated holiday dinners, or talk to your mother-in-law every day on the phone? The answers to these questions and more like them may be something the two of you will continue to discover as you go along because families also develop their own agendas over time. But the subject still has to be discussed.

If he's used to spending every Sunday with his mother, you may resent that. And he may or may not be willing to modify that tradition. The fact that he sees his mother on Sundays doesn't necessarily mean that he's willing to spend every Saturday with your mother, either.

7. Where are the two of you in terms of daily decisions and general responsibilities?

Who makes breakfast? What about dinner? Who cleans up?

Are you able to be sounding boards for each other when you have concerns and worries? Can you trust each other with your thoughts and feelings?

How will either of you feel if the other decides to go back to school or change careers? These days, either of you could find yourself in that position.

In a way, you have to agree that all of these are partnership decisions and not individual decisions. That's the basis relationships work under when they work well.

8. If this is a first marriage, how do each of you feel about having children?

If you don't get the answer you were looking for, don't decide that the other person will change her mind after the two of you are married. You need to be able to adjust to the discrepancy, if there is one. And if one of you emphatically does want kids and the other emphatically doesn't, then you've got a big problem.

There may be other questions like these that the two of you need to ask each other that are specific to your relationship in addition to those posed here. This is just a guide. It's not all-inclusive. The idea here is to have a clear sense as to what you are getting into. If you don't, the relationship is doomed to failure—not because anyone did anything wrong, but because there's conflict in areas that the other person cannot accommodate and didn't anticipate.

When couples break up, one often hears, "He's not the man I married." In fact, it may be that he is exactly the man you married—you just didn't allow yourself to know him because you were caught up in the magical thinking that goes along with being in love.

Hopes, dreams, excitement all add a wonderful flavor to a relationship. To believe in someone without their first having to prove themselves is very special. But avoiding looking at what's real when the time comes because we don't know the right questions to ask or because we don't want to face the implications of the answers we get isn't fair to anybody, including ourselves.

SENDING THE MESSAGE YOU INTENDED TO SEND

To build a successful relationship and to have the discussions that are being recommended here, you need to be sure that the message sent is the message received. Here again, if you grew up in a family where there was no empathy, you may exhibit certain behaviors that will not be interpreted as you intend them. The misunderstandings that arise as a result can create serious problems in a relationship. People respond to behavior—not to underlying feelings. If you yell at me because I'm not taking my medication, I will back away from the reprimand. I won't appreciate your underlying caring and fear that something will happen to me if I don't take care of myself.

1. Misunderstandings over fear of abandonment.

For example, because of the inconsistent nurture showed you by your parents, your fears of abandonment may cause you to be very possessive in a relationship. You may not want to let the other person out of your sight. You may not even want him to have an evening home alone for fear that you will never hear from him or her again. Because of your past, these fears are very big within you and can overwhelm you.

However, the other person will react to your behavior by feeling suffocated and respond by pushing you away. This will make you panic even more. Therefore, discussions need to be had around the fact that this behavior occurs out of fear and around the question of how that fear can be accommodated.

2. Misunderstandings over fear of being found out.

Another behavior that can get in the way of a relationship is jealousy. Many of you may be very jealous because you are afraid of being found out. Because you feel so unworthy, you feel that anyone else is better than you are. Therefore your partner would naturally want anyone else but you, so you spend your days in constant fear that someone else will cross his path. As a result, you come across as a very jealous person. No matter how attractive, interesting, well-dressed or sexual you are, you do not see yourself in this way. And in fact, you believe that your partner will find anybody else he comes in contact with more interesting, attractive and desirable than you are.

Since your partner does not know the origins of this jealous attitude, it is not unusual for him to respond as if the issue you were presenting is a trust issue and question whether or not he or she wants to have a relationship with a person who doesn't trust him.

The reality here, though, is that trust has nothing to do with your behavior. It's a fear of being found out. Having anyone at all within eyeshot increases the risk that someone will see how thin your facade is. It will be difficult for you to expose your perceived weakness. All of this is difficult. But it must all be done in order to have a successful relationship.

3. Misunderstandings over extreme attention to personal appearance.

Many of you will also be over-attentive to your personal appearance. This need comes from a sense of not particularly wanting to look as your parent looked when he or she got sloppy drunk or didn't get dressed because he or she was depressed. And it will translate into a present sense of, "I must look like I'm together at all times, and if everything about me is not perfectly in place, then I'm a mess." Even though it doesn't come from vanity but desire to look 'okay,' in a relationship, this attitude is perceived as vain. You might spend two hours getting ready to go out while your partner would have been just as happy if you'd stayed the way you were before you started to get ready.

4. Misunderstandings that arise from a fragile sense of self.

If you grew up in a family where you were not encouraged to express your thoughts, feelings or ideas, or in a family where you were constantly dismissed, it is not unusual for you to have a very illusive sense of yourself. It is not unusual for you to feel as though you will lose yourself in a relationship. It is not unusual for you to feel that if you are involved with somebody else, you will forget all about yourself and focus entirely on them. This fear of loss of sense of self will leave you to hang on very tightly to what you believe to be your warmth, needs and desires.

You can be very tenacious about this because this feeling is such a delicate one for you. It can be so delicate that your partner ends up believing that you are actually a very self-centered person who does not consider his or her feelings or thoughts or ideas to be at all important. Once again, you need to talk about what's really going on.

5. Misunderstandings over social panic.

If your family was isolated or anti-social and you did not develop the tools to interact with other people in a social setting, you may panic at having to interact socially and literally freeze up. Because you do not show this panic but keep it all inside, someone looking at you from the outside could interpret you as being aloof and above it all. I had a client that people used to call "The Ice Queen" upon meeting her for the first time. These people thought she was being aloof, whereas in fact she was literally frozen to the spot.

6. Misunderstandings over confusion about boundaries.

If you grew up in a family where boundaries were not respected, it is difficult for you to know what the appropriate give and take is in a relationship. As a result, you may not do your share. But more often, you will tend to be overly attentive: you will do all the planning. Or you'll say, "Let's have dinner at my place and you don't have to bring anything and you don't have to help clean up." You have to take charge of the relationship and anticipate the other person's every whim and need.

At first others really feel flattered by this attention. But after a while, the other person begins to wonder what it is you are going to expect in return.

The truth is, if you really do get nothing back, after a while you'll begin to resent it. Yet, quite often before that happens, the other person will already have been scared off.

7. Misunderstandings over anxiety.

You may tend to be either late or super early for things. Because you don't know how to pace yourself in terms of how long it takes to reach a destination, or you are unable to plan, you find yourself in a state of high anxiety. Or you keep changing your clothes because you're so nervous you can't satisfy yourself. Your partner will not recognize your state of anxiety because most people consider other people who are inappropriately late or super early to be passive-aggressive, that is, that the lateness or earliness is intended as a punishment. As a result, the other person will tend to tell you, "You know I hate going to a movie late or being the last person to get to a party. If you really cared about me you would make an effort to be there on time." In fact, the effort was truly made but you couldn't pull it off.

On the other end of the spectrum, people are embarrassed and inconvenienced when other people get to their house super early—they aren't dressed, they haven't picked up the living room yet, it throws them off their rhythm. It's a boundary issue. Your partner will be very sensitive to that issue.

8. Misunderstandings over obsessive-compulsiveness concerning the daily details of your life together.

Many of you will be obsessive-compulsive in a relationship, so you will take care of whatever logistics need to be taken care of between the couple. This comes from an early history of knowing that if you didn't do it, it wouldn't get done or that if you asked someone else to do it, it wouldn't get done properly. So by the time you get to adulthood it's almost a knee-jerk reaction. You're the one who always makes the restaurant reservation and decides where to go on vacation and sends out all the Christmas cards without thinking to consult your partner first on either the list or the messages.

The response of the other person to this obsessive-compulsive behavior is to wonder if you think they're incompetent; and it is difficult to be in a relationship with someone whom you suspect is incompetent. Once again, this is a case where the message received is not the message sent.

9. Misunderstandings over inflexibility.

If as a child you were constantly disappointed and lived a life of unfulfilled promises, in a relationship you will tend to be rigid and inflexible. And even if the new plan is far superior to the old plan, when someone changes plans on you it will be very difficult for you to manage. Every muscle in your body will tighten.

Keep in mind, however, that in this case your partner's response to you will not be based on your childhood fear of disappointment. Your partner will respond by becoming very defensive and your behavior will also tend to take the spontaneity out of the relationship: "This is the last time I try and surprise you. I thought it would be fun if we drove to Connecticut instead of going to the same old movie."

10. Misunderstandings over people pleasing.

You may tend to be what we call a people pleaser. The people pleasing comes from wanting to be liked: "If I agree with everything you say, then maybe you will like me." It comes from having difficulty with making decisions and from a fear of conflict: "If I disagree with you, you might be angry with me and I have no idea how to manage that." Your partner's response to this behavior will be to find you indecisive and believe that the responsibility is not shared in the relationship.

Constantly making statements like, "Wherever you want to go is fine with me," is a cop-out. It's not offering the person a choice.

11. Misunderstandings over lack of expression of feelings.

Many people who grew up in repressed families have a lack of affect. That is, they are unable to show or express feelings. From the outside, lack of affect looks even more serious because it appears as an emotional flatness.

Lack of affect comes from not being in touch with your feelings, not knowing how to share feelings and, quite often, from panic at being involved in a relationship. The response of the other person to your lack of affect, regardless of the basis for it, is that you don't care. So if your feelings are not expressed to the other person, even though you care very deeply, your behavior will be interpreted as not caring.

If you care about me and do not demonstrate it through word and deed, your caring does not have much value to me.

12. Misunderstandings over extreme independence.

Many of you will show extreme independence in a relationship, i.e., "It's fine, I don't need your help, I will do it by myself. In fact, it's much easier for me to do it without anybody else." This attitude doesn't come from really wanting to be independent, but from a fear of being disappointed: If I don't ask you for anything, then you can't let me down.

But the other person in the relationship will not respond to your fear of being disappointed. They will respond more to the idea that you don't need them, and it's very tough to be in a relationship with someone you believe doesn't need you because relationships are largely about mutual needing. And there is nothing wrong with that. People get pleasure out of doing things for those they care about.

SO HOW DO YOU HAVE THE CONVERSATION?

First, you have to make sure the two of you are having the same conversation. You cannot assume that the other person knows what you mean by what you say.

In every conversation, particularly a dialogue between two people trying to solve a problem, there are a number of things going on. The first thing going on is the way that I react when I say what I'm saying. Then there is the way that you feel when you hear it. Because I am acting so much of the time, even if I'm nervous when I say it, I may appear very relaxed. And then, even if you're uncomfortable about hearing what I have to say, you may still appear to be very comfortable and in control.

This is why it's important to share with each other the fact that working out problems is not easy, and that, frankly, you're scared to death. It is important to acknowledge that working out a problem is a new exercise and you're terribly fearful that you will do it wrong.

In talking about a problem, it is important that both of you get all of your feelings on the table in a non-defensive way. If I am upset because you are an hour late for an event that was very important to me, you need to hear me out and you need to hear what that means to me, not only in the present if I was embarrassed in front of my friends, but also what that means to me in the past if I have a history of people I care about not doing what they said they were going to do. You need to let me take as much time as I need to get it out. An apology too soon or "I hear you" too soon leaves the other person frustrated and is really just a way of cutting them off.

And I need to listen to you. I need to listen as you tell me how ordinarily you're never late, but this particular time you got caught in a traffic jam and decided not to call because you thought that making the phone call, since a phone wasn't handy, would make it even later. Or I need to listen as you tell me that being late has been a problem for you your whole life, and that the two of us have to work out ways to change that behavior together.

These conversations are a critical part of any relationship. One can never assume another person's motives or how the other person is feeling. Even if we know the other person well enough that any assumption we make will be valid, it is important not to play both parts in a relationship and to let each person share their thoughts and feelings. Even if I know what you are going to say when you say it, it makes the relationship closer.

Some of these discussions will be very joyous. Some will be very painful. All will be very difficult, if only because having a meaningful dialogue with another person is a new experience for you. And that cannot help but trigger feelings of an early loss of this kind of involvement with people you care about. The deprivation feels awful, but it no longer has to continue. That was then—this is now.

Even if you are angry, be really clear not to name-call. And also be really clear that if you need to yell, the other person has the same right. Sometimes couples are terrified that discussing an area where they are in conflict will cause the other person to leave, so they hold hands and reassure each other even though they're in disagreement. Because I disagree with you doesn't mean I don't love you. Frankly, why spend energy to be angry with someone who has no meaning to you?

Sometimes couples can't face each other when they're in these dialogues, and there's nothing wrong with taking a walk while you are talking. Sometimes you may be ready for a discussion and your partner isn't. If the other person is never ready, you may have to examine clearly what you have in your relationship. But it may be that you can set up a time with him to have the discussion. And whether or not a solution is reached, the discussion itself will be good for the relationship.

Developing a healthy, intimate relationship is a hard job. It doesn't "just happen" for anybody. And just because you've worked things through once doesn't mean you won't have to work them through again.

There will be many who give you advice freely. As a rule of thumb, the advice to listen to is the advice of those people who have the kind of relationship that you want. Their identity will vary from person to person, but they tend to look like people who enjoy being together. Whatever they may look like, they will be people who are supportive of each other and people who have been together for a long time because it's something they choose to do and not because they don't have a better option. They are people who make you feel good to be in their presence.

They are not necessarily members of your family. Your family members may often be more than willing to tell you exactly how to run your life. Be cautious.

Much encouragement has been given here on how to discuss difficult aspects of the relationship. But because you grew up in a dysfunctional family where there were no role models for these kinds of discussions, this advice will be very difficult to follow, and carrying on dialogues is not something people automatically know how to do anyway. The fact that you want to be able to discuss and resolve your problems doesn't mean you will know how to, or even be able to. Neither does it mean that the very idea of doing so will not provoke a great deal of anxiety in you.

These are skills that you develop over time if you live in a functional family. In functional families, parents teach children how to carry on conversations, how to discuss things that are bothering them and how to solve problems. That's why the approach I'm suggesting to you may feel like one that is out of your reach. This is not so. I would recommend that you take a look at my book, *Lifeskills for Adult Children* and the accompanying workbook. These two tools will be very valuable to you in learning this process. You can also enlist your partner and practice together. Learning these skills will be very good for your relationship, even at a time when there is no specific problem area to work through because you can grow close as you share the experience.

You absolutely can make progress. Over and over again I've seen couples who felt their problems were insurmountable learn these tools, work their problems out and feel great excitement at their achievement. They also find that learning the tools and the process involved, in and of themselves, are exhilarating.

CAUSE FOR CELEBRATION

Finally, learn how to celebrate yourself. Treat yourself as if you're lovable. Think hard about what a lovable person is all about. Be gentle with yourself. You don't have to criticize your every thought and feeling. Trust that you are worthy even if you don't believe it or feel it. Offer yourself what you would offer others: the same compassion, understanding and care. Demand it for yourself from others and demand it for yourself from yourself.

CHAPTER 7

When It's Not Working

Wishing won't make it so. Just because you *want* a relationship to work out does not mean that it *will* work out. Even if *both* of you want the relationship to work out, it *still* may not work out. Even if the two of you want the relationship to work out *and* you have a good time together or are interested in the same things *and* are compatible sexually, the relationship may not work out in the long run.

Many people are fooled into believing that relationships will automatically be successful when these things happen. But these are just some aspects of a healthy relationship. In the early stages of a relationship, everyone is always on his best behavior. And the reality is that you're not even in a relationship until it has lasted a year. Until that point what the two of you have is what I call an "involvement."

The idea that he will not change or she will not change over time is not an idea. It's a fantasy. If anything, character traits get more exaggerated as time goes on. Reasoning that goes along the lines of,

"If only I do this then she will do that and I will get what I want" is also not realistic. It is only realistic if your partner is willing to conscientiously do work in the areas that, if left unexamined, will cause serious problems for your relationship in the long run.

Some of the areas that tend to get minimized at the beginning of an involvement but make life very difficult over the long run of a relationship are:

1. Constant criticism or putdowns, even if they're made in a joking manner.
2. Unwillingness to talk about things that are important to either of you—or unimportant to either of you.
3. Lack of willingness to socialize with others or lack of willingness to spend time alone with each other.
4. Unwillingness to spend money or recklessness with money.

These are examples of the types of things that may not matter to you when you're courting, but will build up over time. For more examples see the previous chapter, "Now That You're Ready To Create A Healthy Relationship."

The reason it is so critical to be aware of what it really takes to make a relationship work and to do something about it is that the longer you wait to end the relationship, the longer you *will* wait. Because the longer you wait, the more afraid you'll become of the pain of the loss. Folks who grew up in dysfunctional families that offered only inconsistent nurture find any life change excruciatingly painful. Ending a relationship is exactly such a life change.

No matter how bad the relationship was, you will still feel pain when you end it. So it becomes very important to cut your losses sooner rather than later.

Many times I have worked with couples around issues of divorce. Even when everything is worked out that needs to be worked out—the financial issues, the child care issues, everything—there are some couples who still do not follow through on the separation and divorce even though they both know it is in their best interest to do so. No matter how much pain there has been, there is more fear of the pain of the loss—the "hole" that will be left that the other person filled, and the loss of the lifestyle that had been developed with that other person.

Since you are so unsure of your own judgments, you may tend to rationalize and minimize behaviors that are really unacceptable. On the other side of the coin, because of your own history, it may also be that you will inappropriately exaggerate the degree of your partner's "unacceptable" behaviors. The key here is to discuss your problem areas with your partner until you are both satisfied. Again, check the previous chapter for examples of behaviors that fall into this category.

Liz loved to entertain. Simon could be sociable, but with limits. Before they moved in together, he could leave the party early or show up late and Liz didn't mind. But once they moved in together, he felt trapped in the role of host and started to resent the constant flow of guests. To please him, Liz stopped inviting people over altogether. But Liz felt cut off from her friends and had trouble understanding the "change" in him.

The assumption made here is that neither of you is willing to change. The reality is that even if you agree to change, like Liz and Simon, you may resent that change on a rather fundamental level. So you may have to work out a way to accommodate each other. In this case, Liz agreed to entertain twice a month instead of every weekend and Simon agreed to host those bi-weekly parties. If that is not enough for Liz, she may have to agree to host more gatherings by herself, without Simon's presence.

If you can live with the compromises, there's no real problem here. And as the relationship matures, attitudes may change anyway. But if you can't live with the compromise, the problem area will become a serious bone of contention. And it is important for you to decide how much the contentious area will endanger your relationship. You may want to discuss it with a counselor to ensure that you are looking at it in a realistic way and have explored all your options.

If your partner refuses to work the problem through, the chances are that this dynamic will develop into a pattern for other disagreements the two of you may have. And this refusal may also provide an important indication that if you need a relationship where there is dialogue and not dictation, this is not the genuine article. The fact that he is funny and likes your friends, and that you feel good when you're around him, is not enough foundation on which to build an entire lifetime. As time goes on, other issues will take over.

Sid met an attractive woman named Carla. Sid was very attentive to Carla, as people are early on in a relationship. And Carla was attentive in kind. But as time went on, Carla became less attentive and more demanding. She would only go to the restaurants that she preferred. She wouldn't cook for Sid, and she only wanted the two of them to spend time with her friends, not his. She also eventually refused to spend time with Sid's family and kept insisting on extravagant gifts. Sid constantly made excuses for Carla: "She was so deprived as a child that I'm happy to make up for some of that now. But it's starting to wear thin, particularly because she stopped reciprocating."

As time went on, it became very clear that Sid wasn't making up for a deprived childhood. He was involved with a totally spoiled brat. When he realized Carla's selfishness knew no bounds, he realized that he would be totally depleted emotionally and financially and would have to end the relationship because, by nature, he was a giver. Sid eventually found someone who appreciated his giving nature and gave back in return. And he also realized that there is a big difference between giving and being used.

Even if the two of you try to work things out and cannot, this is not a disaster. A relationship that doesn't work out has not been a waste of time or a failure. And it is true that working on a relationship will sometimes teach you it's not going to work at all instead of teaching you a way that it can. Learning this is just as important as anything else. Every relationship that you have teaches you something. So it's the learning that's important, and the process that's important, and growth you gain as result of the experience that is important. The specific outcome—whether the relationship works or does not work as a result of your efforts—is much less important.

If you discover your relationship is one of those that isn't going to work out, don't beat yourself up about it and think, "Oh my God, I have to start all over again and how I hate having to meet someone new and get to know them." It is true that all that work that goes into early stages is not something anyone looks forward to. But doing it is a part of the process, and each time you undertake that process you get to know more about yourself and become a fuller and richer person. You find out more about how you relate to other people. You become more familiar with your choices and perhaps why you make them. And as you develop and grow your way through this process, you will find the relationship choices you make will become more and more appropriate.

For a long while, Dorothy found that she continued to be attracted to men like her ex-husband. Having grown up in the 1950s, she believed that the role of the woman was to be behind the man. They called it the "Ladybird Johnson Syndrome." The woman could do a little work herself, but the husband's career was the key and it was her responsibility to throw herself into him and his career. Like many other women, Dorothy did this. A part of what happened is that she lost herself in the process.

Dorothy divorced, and then she entered into a number of relationships with men who might have looked different, but were just the same as her husband in this regard. Finally, it became clear to her that until she did some work on herself so that she didn't have to "save" every man that she became involved with, she was not going to be in a relationship that enhanced her.

When she did, she discovered the problem was that she had reached a point in life where she could also pay attention to her own career and didn't have to focus on the other person in the relationship 100 percent. She began to select people who were able to enhance her in this regard as well as to take advantage of encouragement that she might be able to offer them.

She began to see that it wasn't hard to pick the men like these instead of the other type. All she had to do was ask herself at the end of the evening, "Dorothy, what did you talk about? What did you do?" It was like the joke about the author who says, "Enough of all this talk about me. What did *you* think of my new book?" She began to avoid people like her ex. As she changed, she saw that the people that she was attracted to also changed.

Vera was an excellent nurse. When she was a child her mother had been very sick, so she took to the work naturally. Unfortunately, she kept falling in love with her patients. Taking care was all that she knew how to do, and all that she thought she had to offer. Men who were vulnerable and sick would be drawn to her as well because she was such a great caretaker. But then either one of two things would happen: sometimes, the man would get well and no longer want to be treated as if he weren't whole and dump her. Vera didn't understand what was going on and would say things like, "After all I did for him.

What an ingrate." Other times, the man would continue to enjoy the indulgences she rained upon him after he was well and she would start feeling used.

With therapy, Vera learned that she was trying to stay in love in this way because that was all she understood. Being a caretaker had been her role in the family. The only way she ever got attention or affection was by taking care. Vera started to gain a different perspective and see other values in herself. As a result, she became interested in other men who would appreciate her for other reasons.

This is common. As you change, you start to see people differently. So someone you've known for a long time and who has previously held no interest for you might become very attractive. When you change you also start sending out different vibrations. Your conversation will change. The way you dress may change and you may decide to try out new things. Vera, for instance, decided to take up country western dancing. She decided to test it out because she had always enjoyed the music. Her new hobby ushered a whole new group of people into her life, people who were interested in having a good time and in being well. The focus in her life moved from sickness to wellness. And when it did, things changed.

Relationships that develop in recovery programs are another example of the type of relationship that sometimes falls under this category. Many people develop relationships in recovery programs as recovery becomes their way of life and consumes their conversation. For a while this is very comforting and very safe. And very attractive. Many couples who form relationships in this way eventually move beyond recovery as a way of life and retain it only as one aspect of their lives. If the relationship is totally built on recovery and sharing their programs, it will stop working.

And of course many people are fearful of getting into relationships at all. Because they have such a disastrous history, they feel like it's going to fail before it even begins. So they'd just as soon not bother. I cannot stress strongly enough that if you look upon relationships as a process, then no matter what happens, you cannot fail.

I would advise you to think of relationships as something that you stay in until you use them up. There are some people who become boring in a couple of months. There are marriages that break up after twenty years, and the partners regret neither the marriage nor the divorce. When you think about it, it is really quite awesome to think that a child of twenty can make a lifetime decision for a grown man or woman of forty. And then again, there are other people you could spend your life with.

If that's the way you tend to look at life, and if you believe every experience has a purpose, you always get something good out of a relationship.

CHAPTER 8

Getting It
All Together

This book was first written for Adult Children of Alcoholics. Over the years it became clear that those who grew up in other dysfunctional families identified with many of the ideas and information and found hope and comfort in the suggestions that were given. In this version we are including the list of characteristics that were developed at that time. I hope you will look them over carefully to see which ones apply to you.

1. Adult children of alcoholics guess at what normal is.

You have probably decided that you are *not* going to have the kind of relationship your parents had. Whatever else you may do in your life, following in their footsteps is a no-no. However, you won't get off that easily!

Since you have decided that you will not have what you experienced at home, what will you have? Where will you get your role models?

You got it! The Media: *The Brady Bunch*, *Eight is Enough*, or *Father Knows Best*! You might have picked a family down the block that does everything together and that you think is ideal. All of these are fantasies. If you have any of these notions about ideal family relationships, you have set yourself up for failure. At the very least you will be disillusioned.

First, no woman can, for a sustained period of time, bake the bread, be an ideal mother, keep an immaculate house, maintain a career, be a sex object and helpmate, have no problems of her own and always lend a willing ear. Neither can a man be a perfect father, pursue a career 13–14 hours a day, keep all the repairs up-to-date, be attentive and appreciative at all times and pay the bills without a word of worry or complaint.

Because you decided this is the opposite of what happened at home, you try to be "perfect." The result of behaving this way is not sainthood and appreciation; it is burnout and resentment.

What is normal in a relationship is behavior that is reasonable and comfortable for you as a couple. Normalcy means discussing and working through behaviors that cause discomfort. People have different strengths and weaknesses, so there is no mold into which one must fit. A couple defines their own norms according to what works for them.

Outside stresses will intervene and upset the balance, but you, as a couple, will address those issues as well. If you know couples who have relationships you admire, talk to them—find out what works for them, then decide if any of it is useful to you.

2. Adult children of alcoholics have difficulty following a project through from beginning to end.

A relationship is very much like a project in that it involves a process. For the same reason that you have had difficulty following through on a project from beginning to end, you will have difficulty in a developing relationship. Keep in mind that healthy relationships develop slowly; they do not happen overnight. Remember the alcoholism or other trouble in your family. It developed slowly. Things that are good for you develop slowly as well.

It is important to recognize that in a relationship the critical part is the journey. The Alcoholics Anonymous slogans "Easy Does It" and "One Day At A Time" apply to relationships as well as to everything else. Though it is very hard to be patient, there is no other alternative. You cannot know everything about each other in a short time, no matter how intense you were in the beginning. It doesn't matter that you spent all day and all night together over a weekend. You cannot know what a long-term day-to-day relationship is like until you experience it. You need time to develop a healthy relationship.

When you were a child, you were completely vulnerable, trusting and you gave all. That is what children do. As you got a little older, you learned how to hold back a little of yourself. That was important for your own survival. Now you say, "I will no longer give 100 percent. I will give maybe 80 percent or maybe 75 percent, but I am incapable of giving 100 percent." It is important for you to change your usual style of making a great emotional investment in the beginning. Instead, decide ahead of time on some limitations.

Other people do not have to make this kind of decision. It comes naturally to do it slowly; in the initial stages of the relationship, they invest 10 percent to 15 percent. As the relationship develops, the investment grows as well. It grows according to what both people put into it.

Do not start out at the other end of the scale where you give all that you have. Let your investment in the relationship develop naturally over time. During this process you will reach a decision about how much is appropriate for you to give.

3. Adult children of alcoholics lie when it would be just as easy to tell the truth.

It is important to realize that you may lie automatically. This is not going to be useful to you if you want a healthy relationship. Chances are that you hold back on the truth with respect to your feelings, but not much else. Be careful that you don't set yourself up so your partner is suspicious of everything that comes out of your mouth. You might simply say, "Sometimes I am not honest in reporting the way I feel, but when I realize it, I want to be able to tell you at a later time that I didn't say what I meant." It could be helpful to write down the things you want to say. If you tend to be defensive and dishonest in situations where you want to be honest, write down what you want to say and then read it to your partner. "This is what I want to tell you. Let me just read it and we'll take it from there." You may be able to trust written communication more than the spontaneous words that come out of your mouth. As you become more comfortable and secure in the relationship, it will be easier to change your habit of not saying what you mean.

4. Adult children of alcoholics judge themselves without mercy.

Be aware of the fact that your inclination is to find fault with yourself automatically. Rather than finding fault with yourself or with your partner, try to look at the issues and circumstances and make decisions on the basis of them. If you or your partner behave in ways that you are unhappy with, step back, take a look at your behavior and try to understand what it means. If you can be objective, you will be able to look at the situation differently and judge it less. This will be a struggle because your automatic inclination is to judge. Become fascinated with yourself and your responses. You are a very interesting person.

The more you look at how you behave, the more skilled you will become in getting to know yourself. Of course there is always the risk that when you do this, you may really get to like yourself.

5. Adult children of alcoholics have difficulty having fun.
6. Adult children of alcoholics take themselves very seriously.

Playing and having fun are wonderful goals to strive for. In a relationship it may be important for you to say, "I am learning how to play and how to have fun. I want to do this a lot because as a child I never learned how. If you will initiate, I will follow. I do not even know how to think of fun things to do, but I will do my best to go along with the things you suggest. Maybe in relatively short order I will be ready to come up with some ideas too." Having fun in a relationship is a superb priority to work on. But learning to have fun is serious business for you.

Socializing is part of what many people in the "adult world" consider fun. You may even have to learn how to survive at a party.

Here's how some of my clients have expressed themselves on the subject of socializing.

"I have recently moved to a new city," John said. "I want very much to meet some people and make new friends. Although I want mainly a female, I would be satisfied right now if I could even meet a couple of guys to hang around with. I feel more lonely and isolated than usual, and I know it is up to me to do something about it. Last Saturday night there was an AA party in Boston, which is about half an hour away. I decided to go. I made the half-hour drive, pulled into the parking lot, parked my car, felt immediately depressed, turned on the ignition and drove home. When I feel depressed I am useless to myself or anyone else. It was not as if I could have bitten the bullet and went in anyway. I was finished."

Connie confided her feelings: "The anxiety I feel before I go somewhere is so overwhelming that I continually ask myself if its worth going. I carry a complete make-up kit, manicure set and hair blower in my car, just in case I need to make one final stab at making myself look decent. If one hair is out of place, I know I will not be acceptable."

And Marie had some questions for Jim. "When we were at that party last Sunday, you stayed pretty close to me most of the evening," she recalled. "Did you do that because you felt sorry for me? I would rather stay at home than go out socially. My own anxiety increases at a party, and by the end of an hour it overwhelms me and I know I have to get out of there."

These are fairly typical Adult Children reactions to a social situation. "Let's have a party" or "let's go to a party" is met not with enthusiasm but with varying degrees of terror. Where does the terror come from? What does it mean? Can one learn to react differently?

First, let me explain that Adult Children are not the only ones who experience anxiety when entering social situations, particularly those where they will encounter unfamiliar people. "What will I say?" "Will I be accepted?" "Do I look okay?" These are universal concerns. I have never heard anyone say, "I adore cocktail party talk," or "It's great to go to a singles group," or "The bar scene is a boon to mankind." The reality is that social encounters are work for most people. Some enjoy them, some get by, but many just barely get through them. People who fortify themselves with chemicals are not usually capable of a realistic assessment until the following day. Certainly their anxieties were reduced, but their hilarious behaviors of the night before look different in the light of day.

Adult Children tend to react more strongly than others. Why is that? Back we go to those thrilling days of yesteryear. Parties-celebrations-holidays were all variations of the same theme. Going to a social event with your family generally meant embarrassment. You prayed that your alcoholic parent wouldn't get drunk, or that your dysfunctional parent didn't act out. You tried to make yourself small enough so others wouldn't think you were with them. You worried about how you would be able to take care of your parent in public. You were desperate to leave before you even got there. Eventually, your family stopped going to parties. You became isolated.

Holidays were always a nightmare. You got all excited about Christmas or Thanksgiving and then it would end up in a fight. You would be disappointed and upset. It was inevitable that something bad would happen. Your birthday might have been ignored; or if you had a party, you were in a panic. You could never be sure it would be okay. Having your friends visit your home was an unusual event, so the mere idea of it automatically produced anxiety.

Because of your increased isolation you did not have much practice at social situations. Your parents were not available to teach you social skills. They did not show you how to dress, how to be comfortable or how to talk to strangers. So no matter how appropriate and charming you appear to others, inside you feel you are fooling them all.

You believe that the attractive, well-dressed, charming, intelligent, warm person others see exists only in their imagination. That is what causes the depression or extreme anxiety over going to a party. It is a throwback to childhood, and those traumatic, early experiences.

There are ways to make it easier if you decide to go:

1. Don't go alone. Go with a close friend.
2. Drive your own car.
3. Plan your exit before you get there.
4. Read the day's newspaper.
5. Find out if alcohol will be served.
6. Give yourself permission to be anxious.

7. Promise yourself you will meet one new person.

8. Be useful. Pass around the potato chips or help empty the ashtrays.

9. No matter what happens, congratulate yourself for following through on the decision to go.

Next time will be easier. All you need is some practice.

7. Adult children of alcoholics have difficulty with intimate relationships.

Recognize this as a truth. It is almost a universal truth. You are not the only one who has difficulty. Accept that fact. Intimate relationships are difficult for others too; otherwise, the number of divorces would not be so great. Recognize the difficulty and make the decision that this is a hurdle which you are willing to work at to overcome. It sounds very simple, but it is not. Acceptance is never simple, but it gives you the freedom to change and enhance your life.

8. Adult children of alcoholics overreact to changes over which they have no control.

Harriet has been furious with Arthur for days, and cannot contain her anger at him. When they attended a dance a few nights ago, she put a lot of pressure on herself to have a good time, to participate and to become involved. When the disc jockey called out "Ladies' choice!" she said to herself, "Okay, I am going to be assertive and pick someone to dance with." Just as she had made this decision, Arthur came over and asked her to dance. She rudely turned him down and walked away. This incident took her back to her childhood when her father had taken away her opportunities to do things for herself her own way, and to make her own mistakes. Because he was very dominant and domineering, she felt oppressed. These feelings surfaced when Arthur asked her to dance.

Since Harriet is an Adult Child, in many ways she is compliant and will do as she is told. She makes the assumption that other people are also compliant and will behave in the same manner. When the disc jockey said, "This is Ladies' Choice," she assumed that for everyone there it would be ladies' choice. However, Arthur was not compliant; he wanted to dance with her and was not going to let the disk jockey decide for him.

Harriet had overreacted to a change over which she had no control. Arthur had taken it upon himself to change the rules. She, because of her overreaction, could not simply say to him, "Later. I want to do this differently right now."

It is important for you, as an Adult Child, to recognize what you do to yourself when you react so strongly to a change. It does not mean that the person with whom you are involved is out to get you. It may simply mean that he does not follow the rules as you do, or that he is more spontaneous than you are. It is important for you to explain that you do not shift easily. That way he will know that his ideas will not always be received by you in the way they are intended.

Developing flexibility is something you may want to work toward. You must realize that the desire and the ability to effect that change are two different things. Find out what is in your partner's head when he or she changes a rule. What you see as a personal affront may have a very different motive. It is only fair that you discover what the motive is, and clearly recognize that your response is not to the present incident but to your past. Only then can you begin to reconcile these two things.

You may never be the easygoing, flexible, roll-with-it kind of person you would like to be, but it is a direction worth spending some time and energy on.

9. Adult children of alcoholics constantly seek approval and affirmation.

It is important that you recognize the excessive approval you seek from your partner. This can be a real trap for you in a relationship. Yet it is equally important for you to be involved with someone who affirms, validates and supports you. A healthy relationship involves two people who give each other the right to their feelings and the sense that they are of value. If your partner's approval becomes paramount, you will begin to lose yourself in the relationship. If it is necessary to your feeling good about yourself, you will be very easily manipulated whenever that approval is withdrawn.

What you need is to seek your own approval. This does not mean you do not want to please your partner, nor that you won't feel wonderful when you do get approval. But if you rely on another person for your sense of value, you are no longer involved in an adult relationship. You have allowed your partner to become a parent to you, and to say, "Yes you are good, no you are bad." For adults, this is not desirable.

When you find yourself in this situation, try to remember that a parent-child relationship is not really what you want. If you desire your partner to affirm you and tell you that you are wonderful, that is different—that is a part of any healthy relationship. It also helps you to approve of yourself more, Primarily, you need to learn that the wonder of you exists regardless of another person's acknowledgment.

10. Adult children of alcoholics usually feel different from other people.

Feeling different from other people seems to stay with you throughout life. The sense of difference, aggravated by your isolation as a child, is very hard to overcome. But feeling different does not have to continue to be a big deal, to carry with it components such as, "I am different because I am unworthy. You are different because you are unique and you are developing your own personality."

In a relationship, don't pretend that you are not different, but begin to recognize your individuality and encourage your partner to celebrate his. This will enhance your own uniqueness as a couple. Though you may always feel different from other people, decide that it makes you more, and not less, interesting. It is also time for you to realize that different does not automatically mean worthless. We are all different. Growth enhances one's uniqueness, which does not mean that you are destined to be alone or lonely. It simply means that you are an individual in your own right.

11. Adult children of alcoholics are extremely loyal, even in the face of evidence that their loyalty is undeserved.

Your loyalty is one of your greatest assets, and one of your greatest liabilities. Anyone involved with you is very fortunate because he can depend on you. You may run away from certain issues, but the loyalty you have for the people you care about knows no bounds. Although this is a wonderful quality, it needs to be tempered with rationality. You may continue to be loyal to someone whose behavior is inexcusable. Because of this unacceptable behavior, you may have to end a relationship or a friendship. It is critical to recognize the point at which you need to draw a line.

Loyalty to another person does not take precedence over everything else. Loyalty to yourself must come first. Ask yourself these questions: Am I getting out of this relationship what is good for me? Am I receiving to the degree that I am giving? Am I fantasizing that this relationship, because of my loyalty, will work out the way I want it to?

This last question is a very important one. If, when you look at it realistically, it is less than you want, and the two of you are not willing to work out problems together, then you need to reassess. Walking away without trying to look at solutions is not a good idea. But neither is staying put because it's the only thing you know how to do. Your family was very loyal. However, the road to recovery began when that loyalty was tempered with reason and responsibility to each individual. Your loyalty to yourself must come first.

12. Adult children of alcoholics are either super responsible or super irresponsible.

One of the joys of being involved in a healthy relationship is that you don't have to handle everything by yourself. You can do your part and your partner can do his part. When problems arise, the two of you can sit down and work out a solution. It is important for you to recognize that you are not alone. Planning with another person is something new to you, but it takes a great deal of weight off your shoulders. No matter what is going on, there is someone you can discuss it with, someone you can include in finding ways to accomplish what you want to do. This is also true for your partner, who will include you in things that he wants to accomplish.

You are not alone. For example, if you are fixing a meal or running an errand, you can get help. If you have to figure out something that seems unsolvable, you can get help. You do not have to take all the responsibility. You can begin to balance your life. While you take care of some things, your partner can take care of others. You can participate, which is what a relationship is all about.

It will not be easy for you to trust that someone will be there for you, or to accept the fact that his word is good. It will not even be easy for you to believe that a problem is not wholly and completely yours. Yet shared responsibility is essential to a healthy relationship.

If you are among those who are super irresponsible, letting someone else do all the worrying and caring, another set of problems arises. You can probably find someone who takes pleasure in doing things for you. There are people who enjoy giving and who don't consider receiving important. Many of them, of course, are Adult Children. What will happen eventually is that if you don't become more responsible, your partner will learn to resent you. There is a limit to how much giving a person can do without getting anything in return.

So consider working on becoming more responsible. This, too, has its pitfalls. If you are involved with someone who has decided to take care of you, you have entered into a parent-child role. When you decide to be more responsible, you may meet with resistance and resentment.

Being irresponsible and having a healthy relationship are incompatible. You need to work on this trait, but you don't have to do it alone. If you are in a developing relationship and want to assume more responsibility, which has not been your style, talk it over. You can say, "I want to do more, to be an active participant, and I need your help." Relationships involve give and take. They are not one-sided.

13. Adult Children of Alcoholics tend to lock themselves into a course of action without giving serious consideration to alternative behaviors or possible consequences. This impulsivity leads to confusion, self-loathing and loss of control over the environment. As a result, much energy is spent cleaning up the mess.

Your impulsivity is one of your biggest enemies. If you feel compelled to make a phone call, fly to Europe, get married or end a relationship, put the action off for a while. Call in an hour, decide on the European trip tomorrow, wait until the middle of the week to get engaged or to end a relationship. Once you have bought the time, force yourself to consider the alternatives and the consequences. If you cannot do that by yourself, find someone who can help you. Once you have considered the variables, you can make a reasonable decision (which may or may not be the one you had made impulsively). This is the only way you will be fully responsible for your actions. Later on, if things don't work out well, you won't say "if only"; and if things do work out well, you will know it was not the result of fate, luck or chance but of your own reasoning ability.

THERE IS HOPE

The family system affected by alcoholism is dysfunctional. Dysfunctional family systems have dysfunctional relationships. Your behavior is based upon what you learned about relationships as a child but you don't want these types of relationships for yourself. Knowing what you don't want does not mean you know what you do want.

You need to learn what a healthy relationship is.

You need to learn how to achieve one.

You need to change habits that do not work.

Struggle is inevitable.

Mistakes are inevitable.

Discouragement is inevitable.

However, so is: sharing, loving, enhancement, joy, excitement, companionship, understanding, cooperation, trusting, growth, security and serenity.

The choice and the challenge are yours.